INDRA NOOYI

A COMPLETE BIOGRAPHY

A.K. GANDHI

PRABHAT
PRAKASHAN

Published by
PRABHAT PRAKASHAN PVT. LTD.
4/19 Asaf Ali Road,
New Delhi-110 002 (INDIA)
e-mail: prabhatbooks@gmail.com

ISBN 978-93-5521-135-4
INDRA NOOYI A COMPLETE BIOGRAPHY
by A.K. Gandhi

Edition
2024

Price
₹ 300 (Rupees Three Hundred Only)

Printed at
Sita Fine Arts Pvt. Ltd., New Delhi-110028

Author's Note

You cannot see the mind, yet you can find its imprint clearly on all about a person: —in his dressing and dining sense, in his conduct and actions, in his relations and connections. Looking into the mind of Indra Nooyi is important not merely because she went on to secure achieve splendid achievement despite challenging circumstances all the setbacks and limitations and did make India proud, but also it was how she her thought process that put her on the path to success. A great mind has the potential to make others think and perceive what it wants them to. But this cannot be accomplished without innovative ideas.

Indra Nooyi has left behind a rich legacy at in the PepsiCo and she will be long remembered long for her contributions to it,; and will also be remembered that she has done especially her bit to make the 'unhealthy' products 'healthier'. She has also done her bit worked to make the world a better place to live with her concerns for the environment and efforts to ensure sustainability of nature. At the same time, she has helped the company to rise manifolds and to bring it closer to people's hearts.

Doing all this, she never lost sight of the employees' welfare whose work alone can guarantee the company's success.

During her journey to the highest corporate echelons, Indra has was focussed on her goals and has did not allowed her limitations to impede her path to success. She has displayed the qualities of was dedication and loyalty to all those companies for which where she has worked; and in this way, has further enhancing the women's prestige in the eyes of men who still think view women are lesser souls secondary citizens.

What makes Indra's life distinct from those of other women is her focus on the balance she maintains in her profession as well as family professional as well her personal life, and she made the adjustments which were necessary to make each a part of the other without compromising on either. Success in one and failure in another cannot make you a real wholly successful person. Indra has achieved a great balance between her two domains of professional and family life. She should be is an inspiring a role model for the working career oriented women and they should learn from her how they can do justice to both of profession and family how to maintain a work-life balance and enjoy both.

Indra's life also teaches us that we need not suppress one aspect of our personality for the sake of another, and we can display different shades of our personality together be everything we want, as she did as a professional, singer, philanthropist, mother, wife and daughter.

Indra's business career, for which she is better known, has been driven by a passion to do what is right, the drive to exceed expectations, and the desire to help others succeed. She truly deserves recognition as a corporate visionary, an outstanding leader and an agent of change.

Writing this biography has been a great experience and we are earnestly grateful to all those people who were instrumental in guiding us in this endeavour; we are also thankful to the hordes vast resources of newspaper articles, blogs and digital interviews on the subject, reading which was a delightful exercise.

— A.K. Gandhi

Contents

1

Indra Nooyi: Looking into the Mind

Psychologists agree that a person is the product of his heredity and environment, each of them playing a vital role in bringing up a person and what he or she ultimately becomes in life. If we take a deeper dive into the life of Indra Nooyi, we find that the environment her family played a very significant role; and her grandfather and parents ensured that she and her sister Chandrika got the right kind of environment to grow up in. Imagine the kind of life of a little school-going girl in India has: hair parted into two plaits, schoolbag on the back, with the chasing instructions to not stray from the route, to not quarrel, to not mix with boys, to not play games, to study well, to focus on education, to come back home straight after school, and so on and so forth. At home, she is expected to do all domestic chores, behave well, not talk loudly, and yet keep her school assignment up to date. Now, imagine this kind of life in South India where the main focus is on tradition and education. If you are not doing well in studies, this simply means you need to be disciplined.

The parameters were still harsher with the Tamil Brahmins, a community to which Indra Nooyi belongs. Growing up in this atmosphere, little Indra was facing a tougher time, not because she was not talented or interested in traditions, but because she had a sister who was excelling in studies, and she had a grandfather who lost no opportunity to remind the children that they were safe only until they were doing well in studies. Do: doing well in studies simply meant 'being in merit'; you are below the mark even if you stand fourth in the class, and so little Indra could not afford to miss studying while devoting her time to other activities in the house and elsewhere. Tests were a regular feature, being held each month, and the progress card was required to be signed by parents.

The grandfather, Narayan Sharma was no ordinary figure, he was a retired district judge and a very respectable man in the neighbourhood; it was only rarely possible to dodge his watchful eyes. For him, science and math were sacrosanct, and mediocre performance in them could not be tolerated; and he did everything that would encourage the girls to have complete command over these two subjects in particular, without neglecting the others ones.

Being enveloped in tradition never meant that no attention was being paid to modernity. The children were studying in the best school of the city; it was then known as The Holy Angels Anglo-Indian Higher Secondary School; today it is simply known as Holy Angels Convent. Studying in this school had its own advantage. At this time, India had been free for not very long and many aspects of life were undergoing a change; so was the case with the educational system. The central government was launching the CBSE (Central Board of Secondary Education), and a large number schools across India, especially the English-medium ones were opting for this new system; but the school in which little Indra and her sister studied had opted for the ICSE (Indian Certificate of Secondary Education). An advantage of studying in a school affiliated to the ICSE was that it had a higher standard of math and science, which helped to score better than those students who belonged to the CBSE or other state boards. This edge was going to work wonders for little Indra in the times to come.

Indra Nooyi recalls that Madras (now Chennai) was a water-starved city even then; presently its water problem has only deteriorated over time. The municipal water supply was erratic, yet she was lucky as she could have two buckets of water to bathe in the morning, and this was all managed by her hardworking, caring and affectionate mother. Her mother Shantha is a deeply religious lady. She could have well chosen to stay with her husband, Krishnamurthy, a bank officer with State Bank of Hyderabad, yet she chose to stay with his father-in-law's house to look after the children. Her day started quite early in the morning, with cleaning and mopping the house, making rangolis (kolam) and worship. In India, there are several aspects of life which are related with auspiciousness and are done to ensure well-being of the family; and making of a rangoli in the morning serves two purposes: one, is to beautify the entrance or the courtyard, and the second is to provide food to the ants and other insects because these are made with coloured powders and flour. On festival and special occasions, these rangolis took a bigger shape and were also decorated with flowers and lamps. The growing children in the house took active interest in making them on Sundays and holidays, and this was a type of training in customs and traditions; but this training was not limited to only Rangoli-making, ; there were other aspects of life too. Shantha was particular about the children taking part in these traditions because she felt that education was as important as were the traditions; she felt that modernity in life could not be sustained without a foundation in tradition.

This was the reason that when on festivals, especially the Navratri, the nine-day festival, she was needed to visit other homes where the customs came alive in the form of rituals, food and gifts, Shantha took the girls with her, and also ensured their attendance and participation whenever she held such a gathering at her house. When children are made to take part in social gatherings, they cultivate rich traditions and social skills at the same time, and Indra was no exception. She had to emulate her sister Chandrika in almost every sphere, including this one. But that never meant that she lacked a personality of her own. She had her own notions and interests, and now gradually she was starting to devote her attention to them too.

The house built by the grandfather was located on GN Chetty Road, a posh area inhabited by the rich. This area provided an impressive facility in the form of Vani Mahal which often organised cultural programmes in classical variety, and a number of well-known film and music personalities have performed here. What made Vani Mahal quite attractive for children was that they were allowed free entry and adults were charged. This helped the girls to attend the concerts that were a regular feature. Often, they played the guessing game if they could recognise a raga from the opening line or music, and Indra emerged a winner on most of these occasions. Indra remembers that she had attended a number of concerts there. They went there at nine in the evening, and had the opportunity to listen to several accomplished musicians. She specifically remembers Tyagaraja's plays.

The tradition of singing was practised at home too. Indra reminisces that she had a number of musicians at home, so Carnatic music was practised by family members, or they danced the in classical Bharatnatyam. Aruna Sairam was her cousin, and she sometimes visited the family with her mother, and whenever they were together, the opportunity was availed to sing. It was this musical environment in which the children were brought up.

Indra recalls that she as well as her other cousins sang, and a sort of contest always took place when they were together, in which Chandrika often scored well, so there was some kind of pressure on Indra too. She also states that only Carnatic music was allowed at home, so it could be heard in the household. Sometimes, the impression went to the passers-by that music was taught in that building. The favourite singers of Shantha included the great MS Subbulakshmi, ML Vasanthakumari and DK Patammal. It was an enjoyable experience for the girls to grow up in this atmosphere.

In addition to these experiences, watching Tamil movies was an event in those days. Nagesh was the favourite Tamil comedian of the entire household and his movies were watched with fanfare. I would like to tell that those were the days when cinema used to be a major source of entertainment as a person needed to go to the cinema hall; watching cinema remains a favourite pastime for most of us, but the modern facilities allow us to watch movies within the four walls of our house and a cinema-like atmosphere can well be created too. But those were different days. That was also a different time when it came to movie watching because people could hire movies to watch on TV. Despite this fact, the grandfather and the mother had a protective attitude towards the girls. Whenever a film heroine appeared on the screen in clothes they considered objectionable, they frowned. And this had a deep impact on the girls; even today you can see that

Indra might dress in western clothes, but she is always elegant and tasteful; she never flouts traditions in the name of modernity. She is frank in her demeanour, yet you will ever find her within traditional limits.

The third sibling in the house was Narayanan or Nandu, who was born almost twelve years after Indra. His presence in the house elevated the happy feelings in the house as the spare time was now used in tending the toddler and watching him grow doing his little naughty tricks. The presence of a child is a fit circumstance to foster innocence and affection in a person; when we are in the company of a tiny tot, the motherly sentiments are aroused; and Indra was no exception. Nandu was to contribute in the development of her all-round personality, which will shine on the horizon not so distant in future.

Looking back to her childhood, Indra recalls that her life was ordinary but good; it was playful but disciplined; one was allowed to do what he liked but they had to be obedient; and the greatest thing was that they were knit together in joy and grief. Even a tiny matter drew the anxious attention of the family members.

The girls must be allowed to fly, and must not be made a slave right from childhood. This opinion prevailed with the grandfather and the mother in particular, and her father never interfered as he normally stayed outside the town on his duty; of course, he visited the house whenever he could. When asked what the greatest quality of the household was, Indra says that his entire family, including her father and grandfather, opined that women possess an equal right to dream at par with men; they ought to be allowed to avail the opportunities that may come their way; and the girls were never prohibited to do anything that they wanted to do; of course, the decent limits had to be observed. She laughs saying that the girls were never limited, but they were warned every now and then that they would be married when they turned eighteen if they did not do well; but these warnings were only hollow, they were never ever stopped from doing anything. She always felt that she was under the watchful eyes of her grandfather, though he always tried to allow her free room. He was a grand old man who wanted her granddaughters to be virtuous, traditional and modern; who wanted them to be sympathetic, friendly and firm; who wanted them to be knowledgeable, practical and street-smart.

It is not important how much time a family spends together; in today's parlance, we can see family members sitting in the same room, yet lost in their own dream world on the mobile phones; even little children are no exception. What is more important than being together is how much quality time is spent together. Quality time simply means how much of interaction family members have; how many activities they do together; and when this aspect comes into play, Indra was very lucky. It was almost a celebration time when her cousins were at home; even otherwise, they always spent had a quality time together.

The grandfather and Shantha together ensured that the children had quality time and this was made possible through an array of constructive activities; and these activities resulted in a reward too, though it could be as small as a bar of chocolate; but this set the children in a competitive mood. These activities included speech-making, acting, writing essays, singing songs, identifying ragas and so on. An important aspect of these activities was that they were wrapped in abstraction; that is, the children were required to think of an empirical topic like 'If I were the prime minister of India…' or 'If I had three ears' in concrete terms; and this ensured that they children cultivated the capability to put their ideas into practice and inculcate ambition in them.

The children could not indulge in this type of speeches without imagining that they were the prime minister, and they were naturally forced to undertake observation of the community around them. Great leaders are good observers, and this quality was being developed in them right from the nascent years. Indra has herself admitted in an interview: "Actually I think my mother wished she was the prime minister of this country…She passed on her ambition (to us)."".

This type of upbringing ensured that the children were getting ready for their future life without realizing then that they were being made to do those activities only for entertainment, as was normally stated. These activities did not include detailed speeches or instructions; only they were expected to do well thoughtfully. This is the reason that Indra cites her mother as her greatest role model, because she did things to the children in a way they felt that it was happening with every child in the street, but so was not the case never made them feel these leadership building activities. Had it been the case, we would have no dearth of good leaders. Similar was the case with the grandfather who believed that 'our granddaughters are going to be whatever they want to be'.

If Indra has gone on to make her dreams come true, this type of environment has played a vital role in her childhood. But it was no easy achievement for Shantha and the grandfather to provide this kind of upbringing while living in the heart of the traditional city, where every eye was out there to scan you. They lived in a community where a girl of eighteen was the fittest person to be married, and not only the family members, but also the neighbours and others were interested in finding a suitable match for her. It was no easy task for Shantha to be able to avoid this kind of offers, because she did want her daughters to be different: independent, career-oriented. She stood her ground when she was informed by other women that they were in the process of marrying of their young daughters, and wanted to listen from her know when she was following them in their steps going to do the same. Some of them pointed out blankly when she was going for that delaying Chandrika's marriage, as a delay in her marriage could also delay Indra's marriage.

Normally, in Indian households, it is the wife who pressurises her husband to get ready for the daughter's marriage as soon as she is of marriageable age; Aat that time, it was deemed to be eighteen among the Tamil Brahmins; but Shantha's was a different case; her husband sometimes talked of the daughters' weddings, but she just shrugged off any such suggestion. While she faced her husband boldly, she did not lose this opportunity to threaten the daughters to do well else they were going to be married off. The daughters too realized that what she wanted was to give them an opportunity to do what they liked to do; and this opportunity had to be availed, else life for them would be no different from any other woman's in the country. With understanding grandfather and parents as the guides and friends, Indra and her sister possessed ample chances to grow; at the same time, they knew well that they could not play down the exalted status, tradition and prestige of the family; and they had to do it in a style unmatched around. Indra realizes that she had high ambitions, but she did not know that she would go on to become a great person with millions of fans.

❑❑

2

The Expanding Wings

Parental patronage and upbringing help to develop the personality of a child and imbibe core values, which have bearing on the future life. The school years was were coming to an end, and now a crucial decision was waiting to be taken, and that would prove to be an acid test on which Indra's further development of Indra depended; that was, which college the girl would go to. In the traditional setting in which Indra was brought up, it was expected that she would be sent to one of all-womean colleges. But parental view was different, because these colleges did not offer chemistry. The grandfather and parents did not want to limit the scope for the girl, and so in 1972, Indra joined the MCC (Madras Christian College) for her PUC (pre-university course). Only recently it had been opened up for girls, prior to that, it was all-a men's college. In any case, it was a progressive step that she was allowed to join the MCC which ranked high in prestige and performance and has produced several scintillating personalities over time including the former President of India S. Radhakrishnan, the freedom fighter Konda Venkatappaiah, the army general K. Sundarji, the former Union Finance Minister T.T. Krishnamachari, the governor M.M. Rajendran, the diplomat K.P.S. Menon, the former Chief Election Commissioner T.N. Seshan, the nuclear scientist Raja Ramanna, the athlete R.S. Amritraj, the businessman D.C. Kothari, in addition to this prestigious list, a horde of several other prominent personalities working in diverse fields such as art, film, music, law, business, diplomacy, politics, economy, media, literature, health, public care, theology, history as well – the list is virtually endless. And now, the time was not far when one more luminary's name was going to be added to this list, that was that of Indra K. Nooyi.

The foremost concern for parents about the girls is their safety. Indra's grandfather and parents felt that the MCC was safe for the girls, though they knew well that many in the neighbourhood did not think so. Sending Indra to the MCC was like breaking the barrier, as most other girls went to all-women colleges, and it was an important step on part of this conservative family; the only concern for the family was to ensure the best possible education for the girls; and this required the barriers to be breached.

The college had become co-educational about that time, so naturally the number of girls was far less than that of the boys; and this was apt time for Indra to stand tall and behave like an equal; she had a chance to storm into the male bastion. Knocking at the threshold of youth, Indra was ready to learn and put into practice the values and learning that she had cultivated until then. The college was located at the outskirts of the city in Tambaram, so this long distance had to be covered by train. Travelling byin train is very educative a great learning experience as you are able to observe different people of different hues;from different backgrounds and then there can be no place on earth like college. Her elder sister Chandrika was with her during this commute, who being elder, had things to advise, yet she wanted her younger sister to learn by doing rather than being coached in everything.

Despite the hectic study schedule, the two sisters were willing to showcase their talents. In the 70's, Tamil

Nadu was yet wrapped in tradition, especially in dress and conduct. An unavoidable dress code was to wear saree beyond a certain age into which the sisters were about to enter. Indra joined an all-girl rock band, and her knowledge in classical music gave her an edge in performance; she quickly included in her list of favourite numbers some western songs too, especially those from the Beatles and Harry Belafonte. Like any other girl, Indra longed to adorn jeans and trousers as her band members felt that the traditional dress was no match for western music; but to her dismay, she found that the family's favourite was none other than Usha Uthup who sang western pop music in night clubs wearing a saree; maybe this was the sole reason to present before the young girls a role model.

In such a situation, Indra realized that content was more important than form; and her traditional dress could not be made an excuse to limit her talents. This was true for her too that her traditions did not allow her to think of wearing a skirt because she could not imagine of exposing her legs; nonetheless she wanted jeans and trousers, but the opportune time was not yet within her reach.

Dress could not be a limiting factor, so Indra chose to reveal her talent and learn qualities which would help her sustain life in the competitive world. Her mother Shantha guided the girls that sometimes you have to go ahead and seek opportunity, rather than keep waiting for one to come to you. Indra followed this advice when she volunteered to steel advertisements and sponsors for the college magazine which had the chances of being not published that year for want of funds. As this involved going out of college and contact business people in the markets, industries and offices, boys were entrusted with this task; but outgoing Indra volunteered for this; not only this, she emerged a natural leader.

Indra had learnt the ethos to do things until the end, and not leave things midway, and to do things like no one else has done before nor is likely to do in future. When you accept a task, it becomes like a challenge, and you have no right to let down anybody. In an interview, she states: "One of the things my parents and my grandfather taught me was when you do a job, you have got to do it better than everybody else. So simple it is. You cannot let anybody down." She admits that this spirit continues to pervade her psyche even today. Deciding to undertake a project is like asserting your willpower before the world that you are committed to do that in spite of all the odds that might be faced in its accomplishment. She proudly says that she does not know any other way to work, and this is the kind of ethos she wishes to develop in all other team members, for this is the only way to success, she feels.

There are several of her college alumni who have described her qualities during the college days and say that if those qualities were any indication, she was sure to rise brilliantly. They describe her as confident, outgoing, enthusiastic and active; she could take initiative of her own, and ensure that she completed whatever she took up. She was an icon of woman empowerment. It wasn't only other academics that she impressed best, when it came to her overall personality, she always emerged at the top, and this was the reason that she was in the good books of her professors. She took part in all activities boldly whether they were being conducted in the cultural field, or on the sports ground.

Indra was an image of earnestness when she was working in the laboratory. Wherever she might be, she knew what others around her were doing; she had an excellent power of observation. One of her professors reminisces about her that 'there was nothing she hadn't done in college'. If the situation demanded, she could prove to be outspoken too. There is an instance to prove this. Once one of the tests for her class was too tough for the students to tackle and this caused resentment among her classmates. Indra took the lead, advised them all to attempt it, and then barged into the professor's room leading a group of students to boldly state that the students could not do well only because of the nature of the test; she was able to convince the teacher of the anomaly, and the outcome was pleasant; a re-test was ordered. This teaches us a lesson in life: if you adopt an adequate approach to tackle a problem, you are sure to emerge the winner.

In 1974, Indra completed her graduation, and it was the time to take decisions about the future. With the kind of her academic performance, she was supposed to take up teaching or research, as most other girls were wont to do at that time; but the case with her was different. She sat down calmly and carefully examined her past activities: both academic and co-curricular, as well as the strong points of her personality and interpersonal skills, and then she decided that she was not destined to be a teacher or researcher or doctor. She once dreamed that she wanted to be the doctor, but then she felt it was the right time to decide otherwise. Destiny was playing her own game. She states in an interview: "I too believe in luck and destiny, I wanted to be a gynecologist, but you can see what I'm today."

Now, she was set to look forward to her next milestone, but that required her to move out of the city where she lived under the watchful eyes of her grandfather and the caring but eager eyes of her mother. It was also the time when she was to put to test all those values that were imbibed in her during the course of her bringing up and what all she had learnt and experienced at college.

❑❑

3

Breaking the Barriers

Graduation was over, and now was the fit time to decide the future course of action: a decision that would prove decisive for her career. Indra did not want to enter the fields of teaching or research, she sometimes dreamed to be a gynecologist, but she decided against trying for it. There was a guiding light in the form of her elder sister Chandrika who was already at IIM Ahmedabad.

Shantha was working in the kitchen and Indra sat absorbed in deep thoughts what she should decide for herself. She was fortunate that she had got supporting parents and grandfather, but a lack of decision on her part would make the false threat of 'marrying' real, so it was all the more important that a decision is taken, not only to evade this threat but also to prove to the world that it was not a decision to merely dodge the threat. In the background, the radio was relaying a popular song from Belafonte, her favourite singer; she little knew that her decision would one day bring her face-to-face with him. An option with her was to follow Chandrika, but she had already instructed her to keep away from her. Chandrika had proved to her like a leading light, because she was the girl first ever in the family to break the limits of the family to study outside the city; it was like a great transformation in the family mindset. So, ultimately, she decided to go to IIM Calcutta. She enrolled herself for the PGDMA (Post-graduate Diploma in Business Administration).

Not many young people went for management studies in those days; those who did proved front runners because they were going to lay the foundation of the world's and country's economy. This decision did not amaze her parents because Chandrika was already at a business school; what amazed them was that a simple-looking girl opted for marketing. It was thought that marketing was meant for young boys and not even a little grown-up men, but here was a girl trying to intrude in an all-men field. Doubts lingered if this girl, attired in traditional clothes, would be able to succeed in such an outgoing field.

It is never an easy time for a family when a child is going beyond their caring and watchful eyes, and anxiety is still higher when a girl is moving out. Shantha fancied that she was like a bird who rears and brings up the nestlings, and then the children fly away to unknown fields to peck at food that they can find, and the mother-bird is left back in the nest alone. She had not felt much when Chandrika had left home the previous year, but bidding farewell to the younger daughter was like a heart-breaking event, but she did not allow her tears to well up in her eyes. She had decided against marrying daughters in order to allow them to spread their wings; and now the time to take the next step had come, she could not prove herself weak at this crucial juncture.

All those who gathered to bid farewell to her had many words of advice for her, as had happened when she had taken admission in the MCC. Keeping in with the new situation, new words of advice were also there, like keep writing, get the names and numbers of all those in Calcutta you can seek help from, and so on. In the heart, the family was confident of her daughter as well as of the type of values that they had inculcated in her.

Indra arrived at the IIMC in 1976. The institute had shifted its campus to its present location just recently, and she found herself in newly constructed facilities; and now was the time to create a niche for herself. Confident, outspoken and enthusiastic she was, and these qualities led her to do well in her studies. She scored good grades in international marketing, consumer behaviour, sales management etc., though she did never appear on the rolls of honour of the institute. Her course-mates found her confident, assertive, hardworking, friendly and helpful. Studying in the IIM is a strenuous task, but she managed time to take part in extra-curricular activities, like music and sports. She was taking better interest in cricket and table tennis. Her co-players found in her a tough opponent who had an element of aggression in her game.

Management is a field which requires a student to be an all-rounder rather than being completely focussed on academics. It was quite spontaneous for Indra to take part in diverse activities, and this was the reason that with average performance in academics, she was able to win the hearts of her professors and course-mates.

Nearly thirty years after Indra graduated from the IIMC, she returned to it, this time as an honoured guest. The Dean, Anindya Sen, introduced her as the one whose name could not be found on the rolls of honour of the institute, yet she has emerged to be one of its best- known graduates. Indra took this opportunity to say how mindsets were changing over time; when she had joined it, not many people favoured the daughters to step out of the threshold of the house, and it was a strict 'no-no' in case of a girl leaving the town. This could not occur with her without the support she got at home, of course, not without the customary threat of marriage.

Indra completed her graduation at the IIMC, and then she returned to Chennai to work. She started her career with Total, a British textile company from Manchester. She hopped from it to join the Johnson & Johnson as a brand manager at the Bombay office. This company, dealing in personal care products, launched her in Stayfree, a product which was yet to gain acceptance among women in India, so this venture could prove to be a challenge for this budding girl; she was required to introduce it in the market and create a distinct identity for it. In an interview later, Indra admitted that 'you couldn t advertise personal sanitary protection in India' because of the parochial mindset; at that time, the Indian women were not financially free and they simply could not put their requirement of personal hygiene before men. Indra helped to establish this brand in India with flying colours. And then she moved on to the Mettur Beardsell Ltd.

Indra was hopping from one job to another to seek better prospects, but this was not to the liking of the conservative community of which she was a member; even her progressive-thinking grandfather was averse to the idea of changing jobs so frequently. The old wisdom followed the edict that you remain loyal to your first employer with a sense of thankfulness, and you don't ditch it only for the sake of seeking better perspectives; but here was a girl who was changing jobs after jobs. For the conservative family, money wasn't everything in life.

On the other hand, Indra felt that her life had just begun and learning was to be the most important component if she wished to build a viable career for herself. Working in different environs helped her to groom her personality, interact in different situations and tackle diverse problems. She could not afford to listen to what everybody around her was wont to tell. She had to grow both professionally and personally, and she had charted a path for herself. Two years into the job, she knew it was the time to move on to the next level.

Indra belonged not to the state or country, but to the world; then how could she remain in this city for very long. She did not want to stagnate in the prevailing circumstances; for this, she will have to step outside the protected surroundings. There was a fantastic attraction of aspiration if she sought to go to America, she often dreamed of the opportunities that might be available to her there. She browsed details and found that America was the place where things were happening which could interest her. She concluded that she needed to be there if she wanted to rise to the higher echelons of life. She had it in her mind that she would like to settle down in the US. She even said once, "I always had this urge, this desire, this passion to settle in the United States." Taking in view all the potentials that the dream country in the world offered, she decided to apply for admission to the Yale University when she came across an advertisement. Her sixth sense said it was the place where she should be.

There was no second thinking about this. No sooner than later, she was at the post office asking the clerk to accept the envelope for the Yale University. Those were not the digital times; things depended on paper work; it took weeks and months before replies could be received. Often, she doubted if she would ever receive a reply; ultimately, she received what she expected; she received it with the joy that she had never ever felt before. It was the year 1978 when she secured admission there; and rest is history. She was a little unsure too; her parents and grandfather had permitted her to venture out to another city within India and this was one thing; but to send a daughter away and alone to another country could be quite another for them, especially for the parents who often reminded that marriage was absolutely necessary for happiness in life.

Indra recalls that she did not know how her parents allowed her to move on. She is sure that her parents had sought others' opinion on this matter. She can imagine that the conservatives must have advised against it, and the progressive ones must have said to let the poor girl go and follow her dream. Two of the biggest arguments against sending a girl abroad were food and marriage. A girl belonging to a traditional, conservative Brahmin girl could not be supposed to sustain abroad as the choices for vegetarian food were very limited. A visit abroad could render a girl from such a conservative family completely unmarriageable. Some very funny remarks had also come, from especially those who had never been abroad: There is no ethics in other countries; young girls fall easy victim to rapists; young people take to drugs when abroad; and the like. One of the things that worked in her favour was that her elder sister Chandrika, armed with the IIMA degree in her hands, had left the Indian shores to seek her fortune in Beirut for her job with the Citibank. One or the other way, she calls herself fortunate that she was allowed; of course, all acquaintances in the US were asked to keep an eye on her. With Chandrika already abroad, the parents must have found themselves restrained from making any bid to keep her at home; it would have amounted to blatant injustice. The only thing Shantha told her was that she must interpret the basic values keeping with the old traditions and new circumstances, for values can't remain static in all situations.

The week prior to the departure was hectic and emotional. While the day passed making lists and visiting markets, shopping and packing things, the evenings were mostly a get-together when all family members sat together discussing diverse things. The lists were detailed and were discussed in detail. Clothes, food, pickles, papers and more. What clothes will be comfortable for her? She had a large wardrobe of sarees, but they were perhaps out of place mainly because of the cold weather.

Getting woollen clothes was a bit problem in Chennai because it has a pleasant climate round the year, with no winter season. She got the woollens from Calcutta (now Kolkata), but it too does not experience much winter, so it was difficult procuring adequate woollens from there too. So, it was finally decided that they would get the woollens from Calcutta as they may be available there, and further, she could buy clothing when she finally lands in Connecticut.

The parents wanted to get her every little that thing that could make her comfortable on the alien soil. It was a good suggestion from a neighbour to get warm under-clothes, as they were going to prove a great help when she would be in the US. There was little chance that Indra would get traditional food abroad, so there were curious attempts to give her especially those things which she would not get, like pickle, but then packing such spicy food could prove a disaster to the accompanying clothes. Indra had finally made up her mind that she would initially mould herself as per the new circumstances, following the edict: 'When in Rome, do as the Romans do"; and then go on to make a bid at moulding the destination place as per her own.

The last leg of her preparation for the journey included visits to several temples where Shantha would carry rich prasadam and pray for the safety and happiness of her family. Though these visits were particularly aimed at Indra's well-being, it could not be possible for Shantha to not was also remembering Chandrika.

Soon, the family visited the Bombay Airport to bid her goodbye. As the aircraft took to the wings, her thoughts mingled with one another; one minute she thought of her parents and grandfather, how they loved her, how well they cared for her; and another minute of all the prospects that she might have in the US.

Indra believes in destiny, as we have told you earlier; her destiny brought her to the place where she could realize her ambitions. She was not destined to become a gynecologist which she wanted to be once, but she was now going to be in a position when she could arouse raise hope in millions of people.

Next her thoughts turned to what all she was going to miss back home. Her thoughts first carried her to her parents and grandfather, her cousins, relatives and teachers; and then her thoughts diverted to the places she would miss most. At first she fancied she was amidst a live concert at the Vani Mahal trying to guess which raga was about to start, and then her thoughts carried her to the Marina Beach, which she visited with her parents on a number of occasions. Her thoughts also deviated to many other places. She did not know when sleep took her in deep embrace while the aeroplane continued to soar over the mighty oceans, as if it were on a mission to take the girl safely to fulfill her ambition and prove herself an asset to the world.

❑❑

4

Beyond the Shores

When the air hostess announced that the flight was about to touch down, Indra awoke, wiped her face and got ready to land in the unknown place. While most would have thought about the destination they were about to reach, Indra found herself thinking of her affectionate mother. She had withstood each pressure to guard her daughters jealously. Indra murmured a sweet 'thank you, Amma'. And then she fancied wondered what she must be thinking at that moment, surely she would be thinking how she would be able to marry her two daughters, Indra chuckled as she thought looking out of the window.

While the aircraft was preparing to land thousands of miles away, back home Shantha was not allowing herself to move away from the telephone; she was anxiously waiting for the safe landing of her little lovely daughter: she might have grown, yet a child remains a child in the eyes of the parents, especially the mother, however old a child grows.

The journey was pleasant and comfortable, but she was wary of the food that the stewardess served in flight. Whenever she was served a food, she would anxiously enquire if it had any non-veg ingredients. The aeroplane touched down with a little jerk; this was the only moment in any flight that she did not like, she wanted to soar higher and higher, and not go down. This was also the moment for which she had asked her parents for permission to study in America, and how easy she found it. Indra says with a fond memory: "I asked my parents for permission to study in America and they were so sure that I wouldn't get in or that I wouldn't get a scholarship that they encouraged me to try."

Indra states that the greatest concern for her mother was marriage; being a conservative lady, she wanted her daughters to be married, and the problem was further aggravated by a large number of marriage proposals that were received in the household, many of them really good ones. It was also unusual for a girl's family to turn down such proposals. When asked if Indra ever felt under pressure due to those proposals, she says no. With a tender smile on her cheeks, she says that in a traditional family, an elder girl has to be married prior to those younger to her; so pressure could have been on Chandrika: "But the good news was that my elder sister refused to get married straight away and I couldn't get married until she did, so I had the licence to go off and dream."

The moment she climbed down the stairs, she stopped for a while to look around; she had finally arrived and this would give her an opportunity to see for herself all those negative and positive feedbacks that were given by different people back home. Though she could not ignore the feedbacks given by Chandrika who was already abroad, because she often reported negative things about people and food; yet she was in the right state of mind; she wanted to see things for herself because two different people can react to a similar situation differently.

As she walked to the clearance, Indra found herself not as confident as she usually was. She carefully held the papers: her passport, admission letter and I20 form, and stood in the queue. She found the airport staff cooperative, though their scanning eyes discomforted her a bit. This did not take long, and as she walked out of the airport, she was finally in her dream world: America, the place where she was to live her life, though she did not know this fact at this juncture. Her first priority was to reach the university, so she moved towards the bus terminal. She was a bundle of mixed sentiments: at one time she felt insecure, uncertain at another and thrilled at yet another. A new world was going to be revealed before her quite soon; but one thing was for sure: the air smelled differently from what it smelled in Calcutta or Chennai.

As the bus drove to New Haven, she kept looking out of the window, she wanted to absorb all things she could observe; she was amazed at the enormousness of things, be they vehicles or roads or fields. People were busy but there was no crowd; everything seemed to move as if being undertaken in a meticulously planned manner.

In the campus of the glorious university, finding her room was time-consuming but not troublesome. She placed her luggage and lay down on the single bed. A new phase of life was about to start. She wanted to pacify her sentiments before calling home that all was right, and setting her room. In locating her room, she had to seek help; she found all of them very cooperative and sympathetic. The campus was sprawling, but everything was systematic, as the entire strength of students was divided into twelve colleges, each having approximately 400+ students, with independent facilities. If it was a major research university in the world, the credit should also go to the system and facilities created there.

Indra found the climate cooler, but the winter was still a few months away. Earlier in life, she had faced a different cultural setting in India when she studied at the IIMC, but here, the cultural perspective was entirely different; it was a crucial learning phase of her life. She had to learn and adjust to these surroundings, only that will ensure her smooth stay and strengthen the probability to progress and ultimately succeed in life.

Her thoughts once again wavered to her home. She guessed what her mother must be thinking at that time. She remembered how she waited for the telephone calls from Chandrika, and now this task was doubled with the two sisters away and abroad. Indra chuckled to herself when she thought that her mother would be confused whom of the two daughters to think about. Shantha devoted a long time in religious activities, and she must have doubled this time, thought Indra.

Determined to do well, Indra got up from the bed, arranged her things, visited the washroom, and then walked to the university office to complete her paperwork and start her studies. On her way back to her room, she also visited the library. She was amazed to look at the rich library; perhaps there was none in her country which could match it, she thought for a while. She also peeked inside the mess to have a feel accustomed to the new surroundings. She presented a slender smiled at whoever she met on her way, and she was happy to note that most returned the smile. She was feeling all the more assured that her stay in the university was going to be worthwhile, meaningful and enriching, and her masters would prove to be a great asset in life. This campus was going to mould her into a such a personality such that would find a prestigious place in the world.

Then, making contact with the family back home was not so as smooth as we can find now it is today. Today, you possess several means to contact any person located in any corner of the world; but those were different times when Indra joined the Yale SOM (School of Management). Calling back home was costly, and facilities like email were still a pipe dream. Letters took weeks to reach. Despite the scholarship, Indra could not sustain on it, and in such a situation, calling back home was a luxury she could ill-afford. Whenever she called home, the receiver was passed from one member to another barely saying 'hello, how are you' and 'I am fine'; and hardly there was an occasion to talk in detail because of the financial crunch; having listened to a few words in their own voices was the only affordable possibility. Even talking this much came at a huge cost, and she was already pressed to pass her time in the bare minimum clothes she had carried with her. And the approaching winters were going to aggravate the problem further.

Yale was going to change Indra's life forever, but it was not devoid of its share of problems for her; and the greatest hardship was in the form of the financial crunch. The lack of money did not pertain to only calling back home, it devolved into several other aspects of life in the university. And the other major hardship was in the form of psychological and cultural adjustment. Both of these had to be tackled, the former with hard work and the latter with thoughtfulness and planning.

Places and people in different cultural settings have diverse ethos and ethics; their preferences, lifestyle, dressing and level of understanding vary; this is the reason that a new person can face problems in adjusting himself. The big question before Indra was whether to try to change people's conception to things what were dear to her, like cricket over baseball, or traditional Indian wear over western clothing, or kind of festival celebrations; or on the reverse, adjust herself and make herself an inalienable part of everything that was part of the immediate surroundings.

In her early conversations with fellow students, professors and other people, she found that it was a tough task for her to convince them about her own preferences. When she talked of cricket, there were few people who thought it was any more than bat and ball, and for them, baseball was more interesting than it. She simply found it beyond her resources to be able to convince people what cricket was like; and so, she chose to learn more about baseball and all those things that resided in the psyche of the people there. So was the case with her conduct; she felt differently from what others felt regarding the norms of behaviour. She observed people and started to mould herself. All this transformation in her could not be brought about without perseverance but, and she was ready to put in that kind of labour.

Indra found that she could address the cultural issues rather more easily than the financial one. It was due to lack of money that she could not afford to talk to her family members back home in a relaxed mood or talk about trivia; she realized that she could not pull on without some additional provision of money and she could not ask her parents for this. The financial crunch was real, it had bearing on her clothing and other aspects of life. Indra reminisces those days saying this: “When I came to this country, I had no safety net. If I failed, I failed.”

So far as financing education and other aspects of education were concerned, the western society is quite at variance different from the Indian society, where the parents take on responsibility of their wards until they are studying. In contrast, in the western society, it is common for students to work extra time to earn some bucks to meet their needs. Indra chose to adopt this western notion of education. She started work as a receptionist at Yale, and she chose the oddest hours that could be available because she would be able to earn a few extra dollars. She chose the shift from 12 midnight to 5 am, and think of the fatigue that she must be carrying to her studies, but this was at he testing time and she managed well. Why she chose this graveyard shift was the fact that it allowed an additional 50 cents an hour. Indra has fond memories of those times. She states: “At Yale, I worked the receptionist counter from midnight to 5 am to make money. When you don’t have a safety net, when you don’t have money to buy clothes for interviews and you are going to a summer job in sarees, all of a sudden life gives you a wakeup call and you realize that you have got to work extremely hard to make it happen in this country for you.”

Shortage of funds had other implications too. With her ‘earn while you learn’ tactic, she was able to manage her immediate expenses, but was not able to manage funds with which she could manage clothes that she could wear during business meetings and interviews. This too proved to be a learning experience for her. Once when she was required to appear for an interview, she spent the most of her $50 for a dress that was ill-fitting, shoddy as well as lacked matching shoes; and at the interview, she felt under-confident due to this, and then she was advised to better dress in what she felt comfortable and elegant even if it meant a saree. She advises, if they can't accept you in a saree, it's their loss and not yours. She concludes to advise never to hide what makes the real you.

Life's lessons are learnt through the hard way. If you have grayed your hair in sun, as is said in India, life becomes meaningless. The more hardships you face in life, the wider perspective you get about life; these help you to prepare yourself for a better life because you know what to choose and what to reject in life. In this connection, she says explicitly: "Having grown up through all those hard knocks, through business school, through youth, you get a different perspective on life and you don't complain when you have to work hard now because if you are not working hard you think something is wrong."

Saying these words, Indra reveals her own approach in life: "I have a different frame of reference when I approach my job."

These hardships coupled with the education imparted at Yale were doing wonders with for Indra. She says that she already had the desire to 'never stop learning' in whatever situation she might find herself. This open attitude makes a person a learner all her life. As much education is imparted inside the school or college campus as is imparted outside the educational premises; there is a whole world to learn from only if you have inclination for it, and she had a good measure of it. When academic learning is coupled with practical happenings experience in the surroundings, a person becomes street-smart, and this also takes him to exalted heights, she feels. This is a process of learning and can be sustained with the spontaneous curiosity to learn even from a common man in the street. Ultimately, getting a certificate from a university or institute is one thing, and doing well in practice another. Good marks are a good source of introduction, but what is going to sustain in life is your actual performance; this cannot be hidden behind your academic excellence. So, both of them are important.

Indra was satisfied with the kind of education that was being imparted at Yale. It was not aimed at making a person a good manager, rather it aimed at making a person a complete personality. She recalls that she had much to learn from the two activities that were undertaken in the university, called desert survival and arctic survival.

These activities allowed a participant to only make things happen with very limited resources, and this also called for seeking cooperation from others.

This helped Indra to learn the basic tenets of forming teams and extracting the best out of the team members. She feels that when you have learnt how to extract cooperation from others, you have already won half the battle. She has often cited how these two activities went on to get her the desired results. During her stints with the PepsiCo, she said once, “Interestingly, those principles of desert survival and arctic survival come back to me every time we sit down and talk about how to bring people along with us. How do you articulate that noble cause? How do you create a picture for them that where you want to take them is better than where they are today?”

Building teams is a crucial task in the present-day corporate world; and it is a tricky job. Indra says: “It is not easy because each person’s picture of the future or where they want to be is different from what you think the picture is going to be. The first step (towards forming a team) is really understanding the points of view of each of the people that are allowed and then trying to craft the new or better vision for them and then taking them along with you.”

Initiative is important, but any project can be accomplished with team, and team members need to be convinced about different things; in this case, communication becomes an important tool in making teams. Effective communication helps a leader to bring others round to his view and thus form a sturdy team. Communication is important, and on occasions, over-communication is also important, as Indra says: "I tell you we over-communicated to our people about the end state. After continuously talking about the end state in strong glowing terms, it is infectious because you get the opinion leaders on board with you. They carry the message to other people and pretty soon you have this movement that takes root."

She rues that however hard you may try, it is sometimes difficult to bring all people on board with you; for there will be people who will not agree to your point of view; that is the casualty of change.

Indra goes on to say that sometimes what you said today may not produce the desired result immediately, but it might in the future. Those who disagree might feel that they missed the bus, and some people also return to join back. She says succinctly: "We did lose people and I would say most of those people who have left would wish they hadn't left and stuck around. Many of them have come back to the company." Despite there being some people disagreeing with you, it is not a good idea to give up the task. She says, "If they have to go, they have to go. I think one of the challenges that we have is to take a call on those people after we have tried our best to bring them on the programme."

When asked in an interview if she felt inability in communication, she admits that culturally she hails from a society where communication between people is more conspicuous by its absence; even in corporate settings, orders are given for the juniors to follow without an attempt to know what they feel about it. She admits: "It was invaluable for someone who came from a culture where communication wasn't perhaps the most important aspect of business, at least in my time." At Yale, she learnt that she had to improve upon this approach, because a convinced team member is a great wealth, and this can be achieved only through effective communication.

While Yale's business programme imbibed strong skills in strategic thinking, leadership potential, teamwork, communication, analytical and problem-solving skills, coupled with her personal qualities of 'learning all the time', produced a personality that is now one of the most popular alumni; not only this, she is on the board of trustees at the university. Paying her tributes to the university, she said in one of her visits to it that the university had successfully moulded her from 'a young, intelligent immigrant' into 'an educated, mature young executive'.

In 1980, she passed out and this brought her double pleasure; at the graduation ceremony, she had under her arm, a lucrative job offer from the prestigious BCG.

❑❑

5

The Perfect Blend

Does it matter to study in a fine college or institute? Yes, it does. When we look at the large number of institutes in India in which millions of students study, and yet find that most of them produced in these numerous institutes described as 'unemployable', there is no way but to say that there is amiss something very seriously amiss.

With her degree in her pocket and an ambitious job offer from the BCG or Boston Consulting Group, Indra was now ready for her professional life in America. Founded in

1963, the BCG emerged as a pioneer in business strategy and treaded on the path to expanding its horizons under the effective leadership of Bruce Henderson, who once sold Bibles but transformed himself and his group into one of the most thriving consultancy service provider; right from beginning, he had an idea for innovation and talent, and this was the reason that he started to recruit from the renowned business schools on hefty salaries, and this helped him become an independent business unit dealing in management and consulting. Presently, this group helps its clients in diverse business and industrial fields to upgrade and economise the operations keeping in with the best practices. A high point of its founder was that he was an author too, who wrote a number of books. many of which are in best-selling lists. He encouraged innovative ideas, and this helped his team members to put in their best.

It was like a dream come true for Indra Krishnamurthy to get a job offer from this big group. She joined the group in 1980, the year when she completed her masters at Yale. Back home, her family wanted her to return as the time was ripe for her to get married, but she dreamed of stabilising her career. In those days, there was hardly a chance for her in India to shine as a business person because of the licence raj which prohibited most companies from operating freely, and was the chief cause of only a few multinational companies operating from the Indian soil. She could thrive only in the land which has become the goal for millions of talented people across the globe; and when she had an opportunity in her hand, she did not want to miss it.

Indra, however, knew well that this was not going to be as easy as others could think. It was an era when the minds were gradually opening up, and racism too operated. It was also an era when the working women were not looked at very favourably, though many of them were entering diverse fields and proving their salt. In America, an American could create a niche for himself if he was talented; for a person with a coloured skin from another country, treated as 'outsider', it was doubly difficult to get placed and he had to work twice as hard to prove himself. And when it came to a woman, it was thrice as hard because of prejudices as the notions of woman empowerment were yet not strongly founded, though the American society has been very receptive and encouraging for them all right from the beginning, and this is the reason that this land has come to be called a dream world, where you need talent to succeed. Of course, Indra had much of this in her, and now she had to conjoin it with extra hard work, thrice as much, to get noticed. She had an opportunity in her hands, and she could not let it go waste.

In an interview, she has acknowledged the limitation of being a coloured woman and has hugely admired America because it is the land where a talented person can shine at the top. In her words: "You know I will tell you one thing which some of you women may not like to hear, but accept for whatever it is. The fact is that if you are a woman and especially a person of colour, there are two strikes against you. Immigrant, person of colour and woman: three strikes against you... If you want to reach the top of a company, it can only happen in the United States, but you have got to start off saying that you are going to work twice as hard as your counterparts. If you decide to get on a crusade and argue for equality and some kind of promotion, you could be on that crusade forever." In an interview, she states: "Being a woman, being from a foreign land a foreign-born, you've got to be smarter than anyone else."

There can be no substitute for hard work, and Indra knew it in a great measure. She needed to prove her mettle and this could be done through hard work and perseverance, that often went beyond the working hours. Success comes at a price of personal sacrifices. At the BCG, she was assigned consulting projects for a wide range of clients ranging from diverse fields, including industries, suppliers and retailers. As her range of experience grew and climbed up the stairs of hierarchy, she kept working in the way she believed in right from the beginning, that was, to accomplish things in a way 'that no one could do'. She states: "…I have always used that simple rule that whatever I did, I had to produce an output that was so much better than what somebody else did. So I would work extra hard at it. More hours, yes. More sacrifices and trade-offs, yes."

Indra firmly believes in this ideology and boldly says that she likes to make a journey this way, and says that she doesn't 'know any other journey'. This style of working demanded of her to put in extra hours, which did not permit her to have 'the cushy life' and she rarely got a chance to 'go home to watch the 6 o'clock news". And the good thing is that when you work hard, you get noticed for your spirits, and with it come the rewards: in hordes.

She worked in the BCG for six years and became the Director of International Corporate Strategy Projects. In the times to come, she was to join the Motorola as business development executive for its automotive and industrial electronics group, and she rose to be its vice president and director of corporate strategy and planning before she quit to join the PepsiCo in 1994.

In her career growth, Indra had evolved a success formula for herself which she calls 5-Cs: competence, confidence and courage, communication skills, compass and conscience. She states: "You must acquire a hip-pocket skill which you are known for, and keep working at it. Confidence and courage go together. Unless you are willing to speak up for what you believe in, you're never going to be much of a leader. But it's up to the company to provide you the courage to do so, by not shooting you down every time you do speak up. Communication skills, both oral and written, are really important. Integrity must be at the root of everything you do, and people have got to know that they can take what you say to the bank. You have got to be the company's conscience." There is a lesson from the 5-Cs for the young professionals that she advocates.

Her The career had been moving in the right direction for Indra, but her parents were growing more eager about her marriage. Now, each phone call inevitably included a talk on the options. Being a conservative family, she was often asked to return and settle down in Chennai, as for them, the opportunities for her were satisfactory; but Indra did not think so. She knew that it was the US where she could rise to great heights, and was not willing to abandon the US. The basic ethos of the family once again found ways to help her. The family had right from the beginning threatened her on scores of times to 'marry her off at eighteen', but had never implemented that threat; she was allowed to do what she felt like, and this time once again, the family was out to find options.

The family noticed that there were a large number of Indians heading to America, and the number of young men leaving the Indian shores was sizeable. It had also seen that a large number of young men returned to the country to marry and then take off their brides to settle down. An option was in their eye, and now they had to look for a suitable boy to match the talented girl. Despite her high career, Indra found herself to be a conservative Indian woman, who could not go against the wishes of her parents. How could she, because it was ere they who had motivated her to go ahead and had never executed their threat to marry her.

For a son or daughter to be married with the parental consent is considered to be a matter of honour for a family in India, and Indra knew this well. If she did otherwise, she could shatter the dreams of her beloved family. Many young people feel that we Indians are 'prone to judge' anyone even today, and the society was a bit more close-knitted in the nineties. At the same time, this was an obvious fact too that finding a groom to match her career prospects was not so easy as might be thought, though her family was reputed and resourceful. Indra too was a perfect blend of tradition and modernity; if she took active interest in Indian classical music, she was also at ease with the western music and was a member of a rock band in college. It was more important to be an Indian first, because that was an important identity, and all other identities were subservient to it.

As a consultant, Indra had become habituated to give solution to her clients of enormous extent, so she too looked around. She also realized that she needed a husband who would be supportive of her accomplishments because she was likely to do excellently, and could one day be the shining star on the business horizon. If she had a husband who would sulk in the dark shadows of her success, it would only ruin her family life, which she would never like to happen. She was fortunate in this respect as she happened to meet Rajkishan Nooyi in the US. His support to his wife is acknowledged in the media who went on to sacrifice his job and become a business consultant in order to be more available to his wife and family.

When Indra shot to fame with her appointment as the CEO of the PepsiCo, a wave of curiosity spread about the surname 'Nooyi' because it was not much known either in India or in the western world. With this started a streak of wild guesses. Not many had heard this surname. Many people wondered if it was a Tamil surname, but nothing could be confirmed. Finally, it was revealed that the Nooyi surname belonged to a village named Gurupur in Karnataka near Mangalore. It is a common surname there. The Nooyi family is well known in Gurupur. Raj's mother is deeply religious like Indra's, so she found a ready bond with her. In India, a wedding is a family affair, and it is seen as the marriage of the two families. The wedding was like fulfillment for Shantha who had made the double achievement. She had groomed Indra successfully into a business woman as well as into a married successful wife.

A graduate from the University of Mysore, Raj was an engineer by profession, working in the field of electronics and communication engineering. He migrated to the US, did his MS in industrial engineering from the University of Texas, an MBA did his masters in business administration from the University of Chicago and started work with the Eaton Corporation in its manufacturing operations where he worked from 1978 to 1983. After this, he became the manager operations at the HP (Hewlett-Packard) Company until 1990. He once again hopped to the Pittiglio Rabin Todd & McGrath, a management firm, where he stayed as the director from 1991 to 2001. He also served as the director of the Innovex Inc., from 2002 to July 2006. He then joined the AmSoft Systems as the President. This company provides custom solutions and services in the area of e-business, news media and WAP solutions. It also provides services that include software development, architecture design and re-engineering.

The marriage between Indra and Raj K. Nooyi had a was held in a traditional flavour wedding complete with all rituals in 1981. As their careers were important for both of Indra and Raj, they talked for long had long talks before entering the nuptial knot. In an interview, Raj said that the key to the discussion was to make sure that the careers of both of them had to be given equal importance. In his words: "We all have to develop adaptation strategies, because if we don't, we're going to start feeling resentful or angry with whatever is happening around us. Indra too unfolds the key to happiness and contentment in the family. She says that she is a mother and wife when she is within the four walls of the house. Her mother Shantha advised her to leave the crown in the garage whenever she was back home. Indra says with a broad smile: "Fine. I left it in the garage." In another interview, she states: "... (My mother) believes that these jobs give you crowns, and leave those crowns in the garage when you come home." She further advised: "Don't try to pretend that you're still the big boss, because you're not."

The 'crown' anecdote has an interesting episode. One day, Indra returned home late at about 10 pm, she was tired and happy; in fact, as a reward for the successful acquisition of the Quaker Oats, she was promoted to President, though there were several problem areas in its operation which needed to be sorted out quickly. As she stepped in the house, she noticed her mother working in the kitchen, who without looking at her, said in a commanding voice, "Get milk.". This was something that she would never like to listen to. In response she said, "I have something nice to tell you." Shantha wanted milk first. Indra could have been a high officer in the company, but in the house, she was nothing but a mother whose duty included to supply milk if needed. Indra went down and fetched milk cartons and almost dropped them on the table. Seeing her sulking, Shantha said: "Look, Indra, when you leave your car in the garage, you should also leave the crown there. Don't walk in with it because you are a wife and mother first, and then something else."

When asked how Indra felt when she left the crown in the garage, she said: "Would I have liked to brought… (the crown) in? No, not at the expense of my marriage and my children…I'm married to a great guy, but it required constant, sort of, adjustments to make sure that we both equal versus each other, and to our children we both were parents."

When asked how she juggled her career with raising children, Indra credited Raj as the main reason. She says: "I like to say I did a lot of things right. The thing I really did right was I married a right guy! I have to tell you, the man is a gem."

Indra attributes her success to her husband to a good measure. She says that he is the crucial part of her success. In an interview, Raj was asked how he perceived the order of preference for Indra, and he replied with a playful shine in his eyes that the list goes "PepsiCo, PepsiCo, PepsiCo, children, her mother, and him at the bottom of the list."

Jokes apart, Indra is all praise for her husband. She credits him as her best friend and sounding board, and insists that she could not have raised their children without his help. Speaking about Raj, Indra says: "He's patient, puts up with my long absences, and he's willing to step in and pitch in for me when needed." She advises: "You have to pick the right husband. I picked the right husband. Raj is a great guy and he has been a great support and I do not know where I would have been without him. I would say that without a doubt. He has been more than a husband. He has been a sounding board, a or friend."

At another occasion she confesses: "He keeps me grounded, I don't know how he does it. He has his own career, travels, and does his own thing, but we coordinate our schedules and somehow, we make it happen. If we had to find one thing that has allowed me to do this, it would be my husband. I would give him all the credit."

Marriage requires a person to bring about some basic changes in the life, and these changes are all the more important when it comes to a busy couple as Indra and Raj are. The first requirement for a person to be successful in married life is to have a good balance between professional and personal life. It was also important that one did not interfere with the professional goals of the other; this more so applies to the husband, and in this respect, Raj proved to be an ideal husband. This couple proved mature enough to tackle this well. They built a house like a place where they can escape from their busy schedules. Raj never stood in the way of Indra's ambitions, despite the fact that he himself had to travel frequently in the course of his work. They scheduled their working hours such that they could look after the family as well.

Given scarcity of time, the home was meant to be a sanctuary, meant to spend quality and meaningful time with each other. It was a modern house in Greenwich, Connecticut with a traditional flavour, including a puja room. Whenever they were home, the classical Carnatic music played in the background. The house was an effective expression of Indra's personality: modern yet conservative.

Indra asserts the importance religion plays in her life. She says: "It certainly makes me calm." When there is stress caused by professional assignments, she prefers to leave them behind in the workplace, but being a professional and a mother at the same time causes some stress, that can be incredible at times, and it is at this time when "you close your eyes and think about a temple like Tirupati, and suddenly you feel, 'Hey, I can take on the world'." Feeling proud of her religion, she says that Hinduism floats around you, and makes you feel somehow invincible. This is what the Geeta and numerous other sacred texts profess. Indra says that religion is like one pillar in her life.

In one interview, Indra was asked what the other pillar in her life was, and succinct came the reply: "If religion is one pillar, the other one is my family. If all else fails, I call my mother in India when she's there and wake her up in the middle of the night and she listens to me. And she probably promises God a visit to Tirupati!" This is how things work up between religion and family; the two are like two essential domains of life, one being inseparable from another.

The celebrated couple has two daughters: Tara and Preetha Nooyi. Tara attended New York University from 2011 to 2015, where she earned a bachelor's degree in political science. According to her profile on the LinkedIn, she was an intern with the New York Yankees baseball team and is currently a strategist at the marketing and advertising company Omnicrom. The second daughter, Preetha followed in her mother's footsteps and earned an MBA degree in management from the prestigious Yale SOM (School of Management).

Indra is bonded deeply with her daughters too. When Tara was nine years old, she would come from school and only had to call office that she wanted to be near her mother, and all necessary arrangements would be made. During her stint with the PepsiCo, it was not uncommon to find her daughter sitting with the company's founder-chief or other executive's cabins doing her homework, or sometimes even seeking their assistance. Indra's secretary had been trained to tackle any telephone calls from the daughters, handle any issues concerning them and also keep a track of their movements during the period Indra was away travelling on work.

When the first daughter was born, joy knew no bounds; it is a special feeling to be a parent, but looking after a baby is no child's play. Both of the parents were known strategists, but their strategies were bound to fail before the baby. It was at this time that Indra remembered her mother the most, feeling thankful over how she had brought up not one but three of them, imbibing best virtues, even at the cost of her comfort. Shantha's concerns and worries now made perfect sense for Indra, and she often wondered how she was going to manage as the child grows.

Indra could afford nannies and babysitters, but she realized that she could not leave the child entirely at their mercy; and so she needed help of the family members, near or far in relation, to look after the baby. This was all the more important because she did not want to sacrifice her career; at the same time, she wanted her child to be brought up in the right environment and spirit. Indra says about those days: "Both of us, Raj and I, did not want to leave our child with nannies or babysitters. We felt somebody from the family would be good. So, we went that extra mile to keep the extended family happy, buying them gifts, keeping in touch with as many as possible and taking their help when required."

By this time, the entire Krishnamurthy family was in America. Chandrika had married a Punjabi and her brother Narayanan had married a Tamil Brahmin. With Indra's Mangalorean husband, Shantha's life was like a true expression of 'unity in diversity' as said about India. She could not be more thankful to God for all the benevolence she had been showered with. She was content that all her children were now well settled in life and were doing well. Of course, Indra was doing better than others. The ultimate lesson for her was to set the balance between her two different types of life.

Indra enjoyed being a mother, and looked after the baby in the right spirit, yet she could not just abandon the idea of not being a strategist. Preetha was growing instill a childhood when Indra was about to join the PepsiCo, but she was well aware that it could come at a cost. The growing child needed more attention. She was fully aware of the responsibility she had for the child. Remembering those days, Indra says: "You can walk away from the fact that you are a corporate executive, but you can't walk away from the fact that you are a mom. In terms of being a mother and a corporate executive, the role of mom comes first." She realized that with the kind of her professional life, which well went past the 9am-6pm job, she could not be able to give the same amount of time that their mothers gave.

Raj's mother often came in handy; and Shantha and Krishnamurthy too visited. Not only Indra, but also her siblings Chandrika and Narayanan wanted Shantha's time; though they were in America, yet they were situated lived quite far from Indra; they both were at New York. All three children wanted Shantha's company and have her live with them.

The elderly members, whether Raj's mother or Indra's parents, brought with them intense traditional sentiments; they would imbibe in the grandchildren the cultural values they had cultivated in Indra and her siblings. Indra feels thankful to them for this kind of upbringing. Once later, Indra explained: "Now my mother lives with me, and my kids see her praying, so they too sit down and pray with her." This type of upbringing could not have been possible for Indra and Raj had they been left alone to tend to the their children on f their own.

Being looked after by the grandparents has other positive aspects too. When a child feels sick, a modern mother is wont to seek the specialist's help, but so is not the case with the grandparent. Indra reminisces: "Two days ago when my little daughter was feeling sick, she went and lay on my mother's lap. She chanted hymns and caressed her; after a while my daughter said she felt much better." We in India are well aware of Dadi's prescriptions regarding several ailments as they rely more on herbs and spices than relying merely on medicines.

Modern parents vie with each other providing their kids all the facilities that they can afford; and with her earning and status, no facility was beyond her power. No mother, including Indra, would want her child to face any hardships when it came to availing chances and facilities that the world provided. Her anxiety lay somewhere else. She wanted her daughters to grow into perfect personalities, and she realized that it was necessary for them to experience a middle- class background, that Indra herself came from. She says that her grooming in that background had its own advantage, as she could get rich experiences from the immediate surroundings beyond her house, and in the American high society, this could not be possible. She strongly believed that a child ought to be brought up with a mindset in which she can make do with the available facilities, and still make do without those facilities. This would teach a child how to manage things when they were not under her control.

Indra realizes that it was her middle- class background that made her a smart manager of the resources she could lay hands on, including finances, and she adopted the same strategy when she worked in different companies. This was the reason that she could perform most optimally while spending less than her counterparts were prone too. Struggles are the best teachers, they train you how to tackle life's hardships. She wanted to inculcate the best values in her daughters so that they can one day sustain themselves in the American corporate culture, where cut-throat competition is the norm.

Indra also finds a strong bond with her all family

members, and her affection for her is unmatched. Time and again she remembers her mother, and states: "Every night at the dinner table, my mother would ask (her elder sister Chandrika and me) to write a speech about what we would do if we were president, chief minister or prime minister, everyday would be a different world leader she would ask us to play." Even today, she likes to call her mother 2-3 times a day despite her busy schedule.

Indra's upbringing, education, professional choices, hobbies and the right kind of relationship within the family have helped to rise like the Pole Star where people look to her as a role model. She enjoys singing, loves to play guitar whenever she has time, and also participates in the game of cricket. She is also a Tamil movie buff and enjoys the old comedies starring Nagesh. Her interest in music is evident when she makes all the efforts to visit Chennai in December each year when it is the music season there. She exudes confidence in whatever attire she assumes. She was quite famous amongst her US counterparts for often attending the PepsiCo events wearing a saree. Her qualities earned her the epithet of 'Iron Woman' after a friend rewrote a song called 'Iron Man' by Black Sabbath to reflect her no-nonsense management style.

Despite the stairs of successes that Indra was scaling at that time, she remained quite moderate in her personal life. She never compromised in the basic values that were ingrained in her during her upbringing. She never tasted meat or alcohol. Those who are in corporate world or high society, they know it well that it is hard to abstain from these things; but Indra did it so well. Dressed in a saree and refraining from meat or alcohol often raised eyebrows in the initial stages of her professional life in the American society, yet she paid more attention to her performance than this external conduct. She has been so constant in her approach that even her bosses came to respect her sentiments and often enquired before outings if vegetarian food was available for Indra. In the initial stages of life, you may face problems due to your values, but when you stick to them constantly, they leave an indelible impression on others. This was the type of upbringing that Indra wanted to ensure for her daughters too.

At this juncture, it would be worthwhile to know more about the other siblings of Indra Nooyi. When asked who of the three siblings was the smartest, Indra could not help but smile to say: "Of course, Narayanan. He is smarter than both of us."

Narayanan is 12 years younger than Indra, so he has received abundant love and care from the sisters too; in India, elder sisters are still more affectionate and caring than the mother, and Chandrika and Indra were no exception. They often abandoned their work to ensure that Narayanan's was not wanting. Presently, Narayanan is a well-known name on the Wall Street as an investment adviser and portfolio manager. He too studied at Yale and then did his masters at the Sloane School of Management affiliated to the MIT (Massachusetts Institute of Technology).

Like Indra, the other two siblings: Chandrika and Narayanan have received an American education, and have settled there. There is little doubt that those who migrate to the dreamland are able to go on the basis of their talent, yet not everybody is able to shine. These three siblings have been a sort of exceptions as they all have done really well.

We have already told you about Chandrika in the preceding pages of the book. After her tenure in Citibank in Beirut, where she worked in currency trading, operations and branch management, she joined the McKinsey & company and ascended to become a partner in it. In 1992, she founded an advisory and investment firm, called Tandon Capital Associates, based in New York, that advises Fortune 500 companies how they can streamline and re-engineer their operations on way to cut costs to make diverse operations profitable and sustainable. She has succeeded to spearhead several financial institutes including banks and has shown that she has the talent to streamline their operations really well. Her effective way of operating has earned her the epithet: The Tandonistas

Despite her success, Chandrika has not lost sight of her Indian traditional roots, the value of which were imbibed in her by her mother and grandfather in particular. She begins her day with a light meditation, and has also promoted the Art of Living basic happiness courses among the corporate personnel. She has taken pains to spread awareness about the benefits that the breathing-based relaxing techniques of meditation and Pranayama can do to burst stress, which is a common factor in below-standard performance in this sector. She clearly states: "Knowing what I know now, I would have thought of a lot of my business decisions differently ten years ago." She describes this process as the 'inner cleansing process'. She says: "It's an exciting time and I think all of us are a part of that: that to me is a very powerful form of spirituality. This is about the whole transformation of the consciousness of one from the inside, and you use many, many approaches to change that."

She has found that these Indian breathing processes are very powerful as they help to blend the ability to take hard decisions with a soft punch. She says: "You begin to take a more integrated, more holistic, more compassionate view of things, and I don't think the two are in conflict at all." She says that these powerful breathing techniques help you to know where you should put the emphasis. She admits that she has changed her approach from looking at the company's profits to the issues concerning people, and this has rewarded both the company and the people; you cannot ensure a high performance without a satisfied team. She is so enthusiastic about the Art of Living courses that her daughter Lita got one as the gift when she got admission to Yale. She responds that it is like a precondition for the proper growth of a child that she should be taught how to deal with stress, that will make her take a better perspective of mathematics or grammar or science than teaching these subjects day in and day out.

Chandrika continues to support the cause of the arts. For this purpose, she has founded an organisation, called League of Artisans with an aim to create a unifying platform to provide avenues to the craft sector so that it can build sustainable business enterprises and expand its field of operation. Her work in this field has also earned her the membership of the board of the Indo-American Arts Council that works in the field of promoting Indian art forms in the US. She is also the executive-in-residence at the Stern School of Business under New York University. She has also taken up a number of philanthropic causes, including better livelihood for the underprivileged women, working specifically for the urban and rural poor women in India through an association: American India Foundation. She is also a board member and trustee of this organisation.

Chandrika has married Ranjan Tandon, a Punjabi. He heads the Libra Investors which runs a major hedge fund. She is blessed with a daughter Lita who has taken up study at the Yale University.

Looking at the portfolios of her three children, there can be no happier soul than Shantha. She is thankful to the Lord for having given such talented children who are out to create a niche for themselves in the wide, wide world, and in the process, making a lasting impression on it.

❑❑

6

The Blueprint

Everybody is impressed and inspired by someone if he is worth the salt. In case of Indra K. Nooyi, she has taken inspiration from a small speech given by Dr. Martin Luther King Jr's speech "What is your life's blueprint?". Dr. King has delivered a number of eloquent speeches in American history, and most of them are in the political domain, but this speech is different and falls in the personal domain. He delivered it on 26 October, 1967, just six months prior to his assassination. He delivered this speech to the teens at Barratt Junior High School in Philadelphia. Indra has quoted this speech in her interviews several times. She says that she reads this speech once or twice a week. It's only six paragraphs long and is the smallest one, but is the wisest one. She was influenced by this small speech and is particularly influenced by its two paragraphs, which we take this opportunity to quote, because the purpose of a book on a person's life ought to influence the reader, and the author feels that this can best be done by including a couple of extracts from Dr. King's speech :

"...in your life's blueprint, you must have as the basic principle the determination to achieve excellence in your various fields of endeavour. You are going to be deciding as the years unfold what you will do in life, what your life's work will be. Once you have decided what it will be, set out to do it, and to do it well."

"And when you decide what you are going to be in your life, set out to do it as if God Almighty called you at this particular moment in history to do it. Do that job so well that the living, the dead or the unborn couldn't do it any better."

In support of these arguments, Dr. King goes on to argue in these words: "If it falls your lot to be a street sweeper, sweep streets like Michelangelo painted pictures.

Sweep streets like Beethoven composed music. Sweep streets like Shakespeare wrote poetry. Sweep streets so well that all the hosts of heaven and earth will have to pause and say: Here lived a great sweeper."

Indra, in her interviews, often tells that this speech had a great impression on her and she wanted to dedicate all that she had to the company because it was her life's blueprint.

When Indra received an offer from the PepsiCo, she had several views on her mind. She came from a strategy background. This means that she is not entrusted with managing a brand directly, and she was not a salesperson, as many of her colleagues were. Unlike people in operations and sales, who have to worry solely about meeting quarterly targets and expanding existing markets, a corporate strategist must position the company for markets that don't exist yet, and may not exist for several years from now. This job cannot be done without a vision, which should be conjoined with communication skills and ability to convince people how the vision will work. She had in her mind that she would have to work to make the PepsiCo 'a defining food and beverage company of the world'.

She says that it is quite easy to run a company if you know that you are going to run it only for five or six years.

You can confidently boost that you will be able to give fantastic results in these six years. For this, you can reduce its investments, bring down its expenditure, and run it for this period somehow. However, if you truly think that the company can be run for several decades and that you are running the company for the future generations, or you are leading it, then your thinking will be quite distinct from that. In this mindset you will be thinking all the time how the future will unfold and how it will affect your company's performance, and how you have to mould the company into a new form. In this way, you prepare the company for the future.

When Indra decided to join the PepsiCo, she had this inkling in her mind what the future trends of the company were and how they could negatively affect the company, and it was on this basis that she formulated her working and thinking that the company should be transformed to meet the future needs. This resulted into the goal, the life's blueprint, that the only aim for her was to create a company which could be run for decades. When she looks back at her performance in the company, she is content ed that she was right in her thinking and that her heirs have been successful with the kind of changes that she made in the company. She says that the scale to measure your success in a company lies in the fact how the company is running now which you left, and how well it was performing with excellent features and effective business model and saleable products. Indra says that at the time of joining the PepsiCo, she had decided that she would like to be known like that; she was more interested in what she would leave behind rather than her day-to-day or year-to-year performance, because she was aware that people would talk of her years after she had left the company. Concluding her remarks, she says: “Do that job so well that the living, the dead or the unborn couldn’t do it any better. And I don’t know any other way to do things”.

Joining the PepsiCo in 1994 was like a milestone in Indra’s life. She joined the company as the Senior Vice President dealing with corporate strategy and development, and reported direct to the CEO, Roger Enrico.

In the ABB, Indra had displayed her skills in turning the company’s fortunes in North America, and this won her attention from two great CEOs: Jack Welch of General Electric and Wayne Calloway of PepsiCo. Both of them offered her job. In an interview, Indra says that the two men knew one another, but Calloway made a much more appealing pitch. He told Indra that Welch was the best CEO he knew, but he needed someone like her and he also promised that he would make PepsiCo a special place for her.

Personally, Indra was passing through a critical stage of her life, when she had domestic responsibilities; she needed to look after her two daughters, and as a relatively young senior professional, she had to rise further in life to leave a mark behind. Indra acknowledges: "You can walk away from the fact that you're a corporate executive, but you can't walk away from the fact that you are a mom. In terms of being a mother and a corporate executive, the role of mom comes first." She was at a stage when there was no way out but to look at personal and professional aspects of her life as two parts of one big whole. Even when she was at work, she could not be completely aloof from her family life. She says that those who think that they can leave the professional self in the office when they are home, is only an absurdity. No one can avoid to bring at least some, if not whole, of his domestic self in office; it is simply not possible, because the two aspects are intertwined inseparably; though the place determines where you are going to put the emphasis.

During her stint with the PepsiCo, she said: "I love my family, but PepsiCo's also my child. So really, I don't look upon it as a chore. In fact, I find work very therapeutic."

The PepsiCo's headquarters are located on a broad, grassy hilltop in Purchase, New York, which was once a site of a polo club. The office complex was designed by Edward Durell Stone in 1970, and consists of seven identical cubes joined to each other on the corners; they look more like a government office than a company thriving on sugary drinks and salty snacks. If you look at it, you will find no sign of it being the central office of the renowned brand except for a flag near the entrance.

The office complex may look serene, yet there is much flutter as intensive policy decisions are taken here which make the PepsiCo the largest food and beverage company in the US, and the second largest in the world after Nestle. If considered from the size of its economy, it can well stand at a respectable position among the comity of nations. There is little doubt that its flagship product Pepsi has always been second to the Coca-Cola, its Frito Lay division is ten times larger than its nearest competitor, Diamond Foods, Inc. Wherever you may go, market or mall, you will find Pepsi products being displayed with a pride, and if some people have abandoned their traditional breakfast habits to devour Pepsi products, then this should clearly be attributed to the PepsiCo. And now this company needed Indra's services as its strategy needed to be revised to fit in the changing circumstances.

Calloway had brought Indra on purpose, to do an important task for the PepsiCo. The company is and was then well known for its soft drinks business, which included both bottled drinks as well as concentrates. The two well-known competitors: CocaCola and PepsiCo have popularised the soft drinks to such a great extent that when you think of a soft drink, the name of any one of these is bound to spring up in the mind first. As we are more concerned with PepsiCo, let us know its history in brief because that makes a very interesting story. Also, it will give an insight into the situation in which Indra Nooyi took the charge.

The soft drink Pepsi was developed by a pharmacist and businessman named Caleb Bradham and coined the term 'Pepsi-Cola' in 1898 and started to market it from his pharmacy in North Carolina. As he found this business profitable, he set up a company in 1902 and registered a patent for his recipe in 1903. The company was incorporated during the last leg of the First World War in 1919, but at the same time, it started facing problems owing to rationing of sugar, which was one of the most important ingredients of the cola. This forced him to declare bankruptcy and return to his pharmacy business. Pepsi saw the sunshine in 1923 again when the company trademark and secret recipe was purchased by Craven Holding Corporation, and once again changed hands in 1931 when Roy Megargel and Charles Guth purchased it. Guth was the president of the Loft, Inc., a manufacturer of candies, at this time and had 115 operational stores. In his laboratories, he reformulated the recipe and also replaced the Coca-Cola in his stores with Pepsi-Cola. Now, he was actively promoting this new brand.

In 1941, after a landmark litigation known as Guth vs. Loft Inc., Guth absorbed Pepsi-Cola into Loft, which was then rebranded as the Pepsi-Cola Company. At this time, the Loft restaurants and stores were spun off. In 1960s, the company expanded to introduce Diet Pepsi and acquired Mountain Dew. In 1965, the Pepsi-Cola Company merged with the Frito-Lay, Inc., to become PepsiCo, Inc. It was founded in the state of Delaware with its headquarters at Manhattan, New York. Its headquarters were relocated to its present location at Purchase, New York in 1970. The company was reincorporated in 1986 in the state of North Carolina. It has also moved its shares from the New York Stock Exchange to NASDAQ in 2017.

In the initial stages, the PepsiCo dealt in soft drinks but in 1970s through early 1990s, it went on an acquisition spree and acquired businesses outside its core focus of packaged and beverage brands.

It was at this time that Indra Nooyi came into the picture. She joined the company in 1994. She started her career with the company in the capacity of Senior Vice President, Strategic Planning, and from 1996 to 2000, she worked as Senior President, Corporate Strategy and Development. In 2000-01, she served the company as the Senior Vice President and Chief Financial Officer. This promotion made her the highest-ranking India-born woman among the ranks of corporate America. Indra proved her worth when she finished that financial year with four continuous quarters of uninterrupted growth in revenues, profits and returns on capital. By December 2000, the company's stock price was up 40% from the previous year. This type of performance also brought a reward for her. She became the President of PepsiCo and Chief Financial Officer in 2001. It was during these tenures that she took some crucial decisions which changed the face of the company. Enrico Roger, the then CEO of the company, announced: "Indra's contributions to the PepsiCo have been enormous and she will make a great President. In addition to her new role as the President and CFO, Indra will also be nominated for election to the Pepsi board. She is a terrific addition to our world-class board and her perspective will be invaluable."

The PepsiCo at the time of her joining had three segments: soft drinks, salted snacks (like Frito Lay) and restaurant chains (Pizza Hut, Kentucky Fried Chicken – KFC, Taco Bell and others). What prompted Wayne Calloway to look into Indra's strategic mind when the restaurant business started to see a downslide in 1994, which was until then a thriving business. Roger Enrico was back from the sabbatical and took over the restaurant chain as the head.

Now, it fell upon Roger and Indra to undertake the responsibility to look into what was happening in the restaurant chain and bring it back to the right track The shortcoming with the two was that they had never been in the restaurant business before, so the most crucial thing for them to do was to study and understand what was going wrong with it. How could it happen that a thriving business had started to fail. They visited city after city. Indra says: "We had to learn it from scratch. We had no biases, we had no hidden agendas, we didn't have any baggage we were carrying. We just went and worked our way up and down the restaurants of every city."

Travelling over long hours was difficult, but it was necessary in order to understand what was happening in it. They did not restrict themselves to the study of their own restaurants, they also visited those of the competitors. They were curious to find the things that were going in one's favour and another's disfavour. Indra reminisces those days succinctly: "Front of the house, back of the house, and what other people said…everything. We checked quality, hygiene, everything. We tried to understand the economies of the restaurant business…Then we tried to understand the saturation of restaurants."

Their study did not remain limited to the present times, rather they looked into the past from late 1980s until then to understand what was changing and why the profitability went down causing a deep concern in the management. They wanted to know if it was a common trend with the entire industry or if it was due to the way their restaurants operated. The conclusion drawn put before them the exact picture: the restaurant business had saturated. Indra remembers: "Doing this sort of a bottom-up analysis, with no biases, yielded some fascinating results. This to me is perhaps the best piece of work we did in a long time, because what it showed was the industry had saturated and too many quick service restaurants had been built…"

They found a shortcoming in the way the PepsiCo was operating its restaurant business. Despite the gradually increasing saturation, not much was done to ensure the customer's satisfaction and changing needs. They also noticed that a number of quick service restaurants had come into existence while the PepsiCo failed to pay attention to this aspect. This was a catch twenty-two situation for the company. Indra describes this situation thus: "If you built it, you cannibalise your own concept, but if you didn't build it, somebody else is going to cannibalise that concept." Indra saw that the others had already availed this opportunity, yet they were not too late.

Their findings required that they look at the entire restaurant policy and bring about key changes to it. The two came to the conclusion that an asset could give you benefit only when it was exploited in all its possible aspects. The key to its revival rested on the concept that each restaurant was required to be utilised to the maximum. She says: "If you look at Pizza Hut, it only had lunch and dinner and didn't have a breakfast. And if you look at KFC…we were not catering to the twenty-four-hour meal cycle." This situation simply meant that the capacity of the restaurants was being under-utilised, and this could be made up without a sizeable investment; and then there were other means to do as well.

Their analysis also had other notable points which needed to be addressed at the same time; these points mainly belonged to franchises, real estate and labour.

The company owned tens of thousands of restaurants and not all were owned by the company; almost 40-50% of them were franchises, and they realized that not all customers went away happy from these franchised branches. The customer is high demanding these days; even a trivial behaviour point can lead to aversion. Indra and Roger looked into the solutions for this aspect. The quality of the labour force became a critical issue. If the company decided to own up all restaurants, it would amount to hiring as many as half a million people in the restaurant business alone, but they also knew the company's limitations because it was not a big labour management company.

Closely connected to this issue was the issue of real estate. It was also the time when the space crunch was felt gravely, and not all restaurants were located in the best of locations where adequate footfall could be ensured. Indra states: "On paper, PepsiCo owned all its capital, since, in most cases, they owned the real estate." But with the huge of number of restaurants with the company, both owned and franchised, a crucial decision had to be taken.

Indra and Roger sat together and concluded that they needed to take a decision that would cover and resolve all these issues in one stroke; and the conclusion was: Spin off the entire chain of restaurants. This simply meant cutting down the company's assets from $30 billion to $20 billion in one stroke; this decision seemed drastic from the outset; however, they felt that a drastic situation like that needed a drastic solution. However, any major decision of this size needed the management's nod, and that could not be easy. So, more thinking and planning went into the issue. Indra and Roger felt convinced that they had arrived at the most adequate conclusion, but they needed to convince the management, and that couldn't be an easy task. So, more thinking went into this as they prepared for the presentation. Roger felt somewhat downcast as he was not sure if the management would even pay heed to it, but Indra felt confident. It was the first major presentation that could decide what the management would feel about her in the times to come. It was like a 'make or mar' situation for her.

The problem was that the restaurant business had a sentimental link for certain directors, including Wayne Calloway and John Kendall, and their disagreeing to spin off it could prove the solution a non-starter. Indra says: "…so it was the most painful decision we made. We had no vested emotion in that business. And, we started up saying it is easier to sell a business or kill it than it is easy to grow a business, so let's try our best to grow what we have got."

At the board meeting, Indra started her presentation from the other way round, speaking contrary to what she had decided to do. She knew that the better the idea is, the tougher it is to convince people. She said that they had terrific brands and that they really wanted to grow that restaurant business, and not spin it off. At the same time, she went on to prove with the help of supporting data and documents that the restaurant business was causing problem to the parent company, it was like a 'limb eating into the body' situation.

Convincing requires a great skill, and Indra was confident of her strategy. She started then with the strategic analysis of a restaurant business, without telling the board that she was going to recommend a spin-off. At first, she went into the economies of the restaurant industry, then she described what was happening in the industry then, and then she put out four options for the board to choose from, and continuing with the analysis, she zeroed in on two options; and finally, she came to the conclusion, with the board's concurrence, that the spin-off was just the solution. She remembers that presentation with these words: "So when we pushed through the analysis on the two options we sort of zeroed in on, it was crystal clear that the spin-off was the best option. So, it was a very deliberate, iterative process. It was not one of those things where we said, just close it off."

To bring the board on her side of the conclusion, she took an indirect route, and that paid off. The time showed that she was right in her approach, as it unburdened off the parent company, opening vistas for its further growth.

Indra says that the involvement of the stakeholders is crucial as they would feel that the decision was taken by them. About this decision, she says: "Our board was involved. Every step of it and, I must say, the board contributed hugely to the discussion and it was an excellent discussion." She presented her decision in a way that it encouraged the board to discuss it with other options as well, and this was how she made the board feel that it was ere they who had taken the decision, and it was not a fed one.

Her solution to spin off the restaurant business had been accepted, but she was aware that there could be some people who thought that it had cut down the company's assets sizably, almost by one-third. This had to be made up, and she took upon herself this responsibility to replenish the assets. She undertook her study to see which direction she should go, which company she could acquire that would add value to the parent company.

Indra, at this juncture, had clear notions about how the PepsiCo should function. From her studies and analysis, she concluded that the PepsiCo brands were not relevant round the clock; the company had nothing to offer to the customers from early morning to until 10 am. She says: "We thought that as a very important part of the day that we had to capture." For this purpose, she thought about the options she could have. She could have proposed to the board to build a brand to serve this purpose, but then it required a huge effort, and this effort could have been easily saved if a brand like Tropicana was already available; it was then part of the Seagram; the only thing was to acquire it. Tropicana was good for breakfast and good for you, so a decision was made to buy it. It could be acquired in two ways: IPO or sale. They chose to bid for it and bought it in 1997.

Why did Indra go for Tropicana instead of building a new brand? To answer this, you will need to go deep down her mind. It made sense strategically and financially, but there was more to it when looked from without. She wanted to connect PepsiCo with customers sentimentally too, and also wanted to look after their diverse needs. The PepsiCo thrived on the business of soft drinks, though it is widely acknowledged that they were (and are) not good for health, though people enjoyed them a great deal. Same was the case with the salted snacks sold by the company. This was the reason that she introduced fresh juice which was genuinely good for people. She was inclined to draw a line between what was fun for customers and what was good for them. It was under the 'good for you' category that Indra wanted to focus more. She moved in this direction with the acquisition of the Tropicana.

Indra, however, also defends the soft drinks. In an interview with the Economic Times, she says: "I think one gulab jamun (an Indian sweet full of sugary syrup) has got six Pepsis in it. It is okay that I consume huge quantities of that. So I think it (Pepsi) has its place in the Indian diet. In another interview she says: "I eat a bag of Lays every day. Because, you know, obesity doesn't happen because you eat a bag of Lays every day. Let's think of Lays or Fuffles. What is it? It's a potato, an American farmer-grown potato, right here in the United States, that comes out of the soil from the United States, comes straight into a plant that's in the United States. It's merely sliced, fried, lightly salted and put in a bag. And let me just say something…There's less salt in a bag of potato chips than there is in a slice of bread. There's less salt in a bag of potato chips and don't exercise and eat all kinds of unhealthy foods beyond that and say, 'I'm obese', there is something wrong, okay!"

Indra talks reasonably when she follows this approach. In another interview, she says: "The question is how do you make sure you eat it all in one way?...How do you ensure people do not end up binging on unhealthy snacks and do eat the healthy ones too." Indra's approach in this connection was reasonable. She wants to make consumers available a whole range of healthy options too. She says: "In Quaker, we have a whole range of Quaker snacks – Quaker bars, Quaker oatmeal and cookies. We have a fantastic pipeline of products."

To convince the board about this acquisition costing $3.3 billion was not going to be an easy one, but once again, she and Roger came together to explain the in-thing that the soft drinks business was likely to see a downslide in the times to come mainly because of spreading health awareness. The decision to acquire Tropicana was not opposed by the PepsiCo executives alone, it was also criticised by the Wall Street critics. Contrary to the opposition and criticism, the Tropicana allowed the PepsiCo to gain advantage and a competitive edge because it captured 44% of the chilled orange juice segment, the fastest growing segment of the juice market. It was an especially encouraging metric when compared with Coca-Cola's Minute Maid which captured less than half of the Tropicana's market share.

Cola Wars

The competition between the Coca-Cola and the PepsiCo with each other, particularly over the flagship brands of cola is referred to as cola wars. These wars started between the two rivals from 1970s, when the Coca-Cola was leading with the PepsiCo trailing at number two. In the early 1980s, the Coca-Cola saw itself losing grounds to Pepsi and to Diet Coke and its competitors' products; it was at this time that the Coca-Cola decided to change the beverage's formula and flavour. In April 1985, it introduced the new recipe which became known as New Coke. The company was prompted to make this move because the rival Pepsi had a little sweeter taste, and had changed its recipe to make Coke a little sweeter; however, the customers did not take it softly and a backlash followed, forcing the company to backtrack to the old recipe introducing it with the new name 'Coca-Cola Classic'. Though a retreat, it brought back Coke into competition again gaining a wide ground, so some theorists have also termed it a masterstroke, though the Coca-Cola denies the claim. This is an interesting case study and this incident is included as part of business school curricula in the US and other countries, and is a major event of the cola wars.

Right from 1975, the PepsiCo had been making efforts to outshine the Coke, so it introduced a number of schemes such as Pepsi Challenge, Blind Taste Tests and Pepsi Stuff (drink Pepsi, get stuff). Under the last scheme, the consumers could collect Pepsi Points on packages and cups and could redeem them for free Pepsi merchandise. They continued with this scheme for two years as it had won the consumers' support and then they included even the Mountain Dew under this scheme, which proved an instant hit with the consumers. The programme was also expanded to other international markets where Pepsi operated. It continued for several years though its features were modified from time to time.

It would be interesting to quote an interesting law-suit. In one of the advertisements under the Pepsi Stuff, it showed a young man in the cockpit of a Harrier Jump Jet, with the caption below it: "Harrier Jet—7 million Pepsi points". There was a mechanism to buy the additional Pepsi points to complete the Pepsi Stuff order. John Leonard, a resident of Seattle (Washington), sent in a Pepsi Stuff request with the maximum number of points and a cheque for $700,000 to make up for the extra points he needed. The PepsiCo did not accept the request and in turn, Leonard filed a law-suit. The court ruled that a reasonable man would not deduce from the commercial that the Pepsi was in fact offering a Harrier Jet. It prompted the PepsiCo to add the words 'Just Kidding' below the caption, and also raised the price to '700 million Pepsi Points'. The judgement in this case was delivered in 1999 when Indra was very much part of the PepsiCo.

Indra continued with her study of the rival Coca-Cola, its strengths and weaknesses, what worked for it and what didn't. She concluded that the Coca-Cola had spun off its entities involving labour-intensive businesses. She noted that the strength of the PepsiCo lay in its effective ability to deal with franchises, while it lacked in dealing with the distribution, though the case was different with Frito Lay which was solely based on distribution and an infrastructure had been created for this. On the contrary, bottling and distribution operations in the soft drinks needed a huge effort involving a very large manpower at the local level with which a franchise could deal better. It was in this process that the Coca-Cola had spun off its bottling operations to franchises and had given them several advantages. Looking into the minds of the Coca-Cola, Indra observes: "Unlike Frito Lay where distribution is everything, in the beverage business [both] a franchise company and the distribution company are important. So, it is critical for us that we look at these as two [independent] entities."

Indra compared the capacities that the two rival companies possessed, and concluded: "Again we realized that our strength is in franchise business." And this conclusion went operative and convincing the management did not prove very difficult, as they were already overawed of her earlier presentations of spinning off the restaurant business and acquiring Tropicana, which had proved a leap forward for the company.

Ten years later, the PepsiCo too followed in these footsteps; however, effort was made to eliminate all those errors that were committed by the rival company. Instead of simply involving more franchises, the PepsiCo went for an IPO (initial public offer) for the bottling business, which also brought in revenues.

Pleased at what she had achieved in the company, Indra was now looking for more challenges as a strategist, and in her share fell another assignment that was hugely challenging.

Roger called her one day not many months after she joined the PepsiCo and asked her to develop a strategy that would make the company a defining corporation for the 21st century. In fact, Roger saw the company transform itself into the one like the GE.

Indra closed her eyes for a while and then gave a nod; it was going to be a great strategic challenge. Roger sat down with Indra to arrive at an action plan, and then they zeroed in on the acquisition of the Quaker Oats. About this decision, Indra says: "Tropicana brought in a little over $3 billion. And then Quaker Oats brought in $7 billion. So, it was there. We have written a case study on it and it has all the decision-making and how we went through it, but I think it was an incredible financial transformation, because return on invested capital went from 15% to 25%."

She explains that the cash flow on $30 billion of revenue was like a billion something while it was over $3 billion on $20 billion of revenue, $10 billion less. Naturally, it was a great transformation for the company and proved a game-changing decision.

When Indra was given credit for this accomplishment, she modestly said that it was not at all an individual decision. She was also questioned why she went for acquisition rather than building a brand for the company because it could be done under Frito Lay. Explaining this, she says: "…the other reason we bought Quaker Oats, which very few people really understand, is because it was again similar to the Tropicana acquisition. If you look at Frito Lay, if you want to make a healthy product, you could not use any other Frito products or brands. To call them Frito Bar, or the Lays Bar, or Ruffles Bar, and expect to use it for breakfast would be crazy. They just did not have the right association." This was the precise reason that Indra favoured to go in for another brand that dealt in a nutrition-credential backed brand to launch a whole range of good food products.

She adds to this that they did not arrive at the Quaker Oats only because it was a big name. She says: "…We did all our brand studies, and it (Quaker Oats) was on the top."

The Quaker Oats Company's ownership of Gatorade was a positive strategic move for PepsiCo, since Gatorade was responsible for 80% of sports drink sales at that time. Similar to the Tropicana, this strategic move gave PepsiCo a definite edge over the Coca-Cola, the owner of Powerade, which was then second in sports drink segment.

This helped the PepsiCo to raise its net annual profits from $2.7 billion to $6.5 billion.

While the world was busy admiring Indra for her accomplishments, she was busy acquiring the SoBe for $337 million, beating the bid by the Coca-Cola with a sizeable difference.

Indra's strategic success with redirection of the PepsiCo, also called 'Performance with a Purpose', has been largely successful. It involved creating long-term growth while leaving a positive impact on the society and environment. She was making an attempt to not only create a sustainable business model for the company, but also make it something which the people would love to associate themselves with. It was in this endeavour that she reclassified the PepsiCo products into three broad categories: (a) 'Fun for you', which included products like potato chips and regular soda; (b) 'Better for you', which included products like diet or low-fat versions of snacks and sodas; and (c) 'Good for you', which included items such as oatmeal. The company too looked at her perspective with a positive attitude and backed up her initiative with ample funding. She moved corporate funding away from junk foods to the healthier alternatives, with the purpose of improving healthiness of even the 'fun' products. Later in 2015, she removed from Diet Cola 'aspartame', an artificial non-saccharide sweetener 200 times sweeter than sucrose, used in packaged foods and beverages as a substitute for sugar. It was also a shift towards healthier food alternative; this she did despite the fact that there was no creditable evidence that aspartame possesses harmful effects.

Indra says: "We can now see how we have got a range of products from 'fun for you' to 'better for you' to 'good for you', with beverages, meals, snacks, and we have grown this company deliberately over time. It actually started in 1996. It was the first time we started talking about it. Actually, I would say PepsiCo anticipated it in 1990 when we moved to classifying beverages as liquid refreshing beverages as opposed to carbonated soft drinks. That is when moved into partnerships with Lipton for tea, with Starbucks for cappuccino and we started moving into juices ourselves."

Describing how this step has proved an amazing experience for the company, she states: "So we started really making the move in 1990, and along with the acquisition of Tropicana and then Gatorade, we really cemented our move into non-carbonated beverages and today we have the number one brand literally in every aspect of non-carbonated beverages."

The 'Performance with a Purpose' has taken the form of a philosophy. In numerous interviews over the years she has explained the idea in different ways. In one place, she says: "It (Performance with a Purpose) is basically PepsiCo saying that companies can no longer perform and toss costs to society. We believe that the new future is public-private partnerships, where companies feel responsible for society at large."

To prove this point, Indra goes on to say through an example: "If companies use water from the ground, it's important we put the water back. It's important we contribute to energy balance. It's important we contribute to a sustainable family if you're in the agricultural business. It's important that if society has a problem with obesity, rather than say, 'It's not my problem,' you work with lawmakers, work with the regulators and legislators, with NGOs to say, 'How can we address it?' So our performance with a purpose is how can we as a company do better by doing better, and that's really the whole idea of performance with a purpose, and that's why I believe shareholders should be thrilled that PepsiCo's in fact building a sustainable corporation, sustainable not just financially but sustainable in terms of being a great citizen of every society in which we participate."

Indra emphasises in an interview: "In the area of environmental sustainability, our goal is that by 2015, globally we want to reduce water consumption per unit of production by 20 percent, electricity by 20 percent and fuel by 25 percent. The goal is to reduce, reuse and recycle." Expressing satisfaction at what she and the PepsiCo have achieved, she says: "I am proud to say that at this point, relative to where we want to be, we are ahead of the original plan."

In 2015, the company slashed the overall use of water in its operations by about 3.2 billion litres in a drive towards improved water conservation. In doing so it has saved more than $80 million in production costs. Between 2011 and 2015, it reduced its water usage per unit of production by 26%, exceeding its 20% goal. These actions were the PepsiCo's broader sustainability agenda, which has delivered more than $600 million in cost savings in the last five years through water, energy, packaging and waste reduction initiatives. The company has also partnered with non-government organisations to provide safe water access to over 9 million people in less affluent countries since 2006, exceeding its original goal of six million people by the end of 2015.

Further explaining the concept of 'purpose', she says: "The purpose part comes in three layers. The first is human sustainability. I feel we have to focus on ensuring people live healthy and live longer. So, before making sure the portfolio has health and wellness products and 'fun for you', I want to accelerate the move to a balanced portfolio globally. The second part is environmental sustainability. Clearly, we want to make the world a better place for our children. So, worrying about the water use, energy use and recyclability, all of that stuff. Again, you have to balance very carefully with the profit part of it, and talking about sustainability. So, everything cannot happen tomorrow. We want to lay out a programme and deliberately work towards it. And the third part is, for our employees and people sustainability. It is making sure that PepsiCo is the most diverse and the most inclusive place for all people—women, minorities, irrespective of your ethnic background or nationalities. We want to make PepsiCo the place where the best people want to come and work. They feel they can have a great career and progress. Because we are drawing people from communities."

Indra reveals her plan: "…I think if PepsiCo could take the leadership on these three purpose-driven activities, we could be among the defining corporations because we would have a clear plan for each one, but we are not going to give up on performance. So, that is the plan and that is what we are going to work against…I think PepsiCo has the unique opportunity to be what I would call the defining corporation of the 21st century."

Indra further explains: "We started off saying when people talk about the last two decades of the 20th century and talk about the great companies, they talk about IBM, Johnson & Johnson and GE and, you know, names like Microsoft immediately come to mind. But I think, in the first part of the 21st century, and I say first part because I don't want to say 21st century—that is 100 years, who knows who is going to be around or what the world is going to look like—so the first two or three decades of the 21st century, there is a unique opportunity for PepsiCo to be among the defining corporations." She goes on to put special emphasis on the word 'among', and says that she did not say 'the'.

Indra is very clear about her philosophy. She explains that it is essential for the PepsiCo to be amongst the defining corporations globally. She says: "We want to be able to work with the local communities and make sure that local communities feel great about having PepsiCo in their neighbourhood. So, clearly, I think if PepsiCo could take the leadership on these three purpose-driven activities, we could be among the defining corporations because we would have a clear plan for each one, but we are not going to give up on performance. So, that is the plan and that is what we are going to work against."

Indra feels that the PepsiCo is able to retain the talent because of its compensation and ideology. She says:

"Even in these early days, we have not unveiled this whole strategy globally, just talking to a few of our employees it resonates. Today's is a war for talent. People come into the company and stay for reasons other than compensation. It becomes a great leveller. I think if people do not want to come in and stay because they love coming to work every day, I don't think you can hold on to that business. PepsiCo is what it is because of the culture we have."

You cannot compete without having an ability to retain manpower, especially the talent. Indra continues: "Getting the right people and then retaining them becomes more important than anything else."

One thing is sure that making deals at such a great extent and bringing about a change in the basic structure and composition of the company's products was a stress-causing activity. Indra has herself admitted that making strategy is a round-the-clock job. She says: "I wake up in the middle of the night and write different versions of PepsiCo on a sheet of paper." After she had tough negotiations with the Quaker Oats executives, she flew to Pittsburgh to pray at the family's deity. When the team is facing a rough situation, which normally happens in negotiations of this tune, it is necessary for the leader to keep the team happy and contented, so that their efficiency does not go down.

Working at such a high level requires a decision-making ability of the finest kind. Acknowledging accolade for her dedication, Roger Enrico says: "If she gets an idea, she goes after it. There's no stopping her." The similar sentiments have been expressed by others who have been associated with the projects.

While the world was praising her, Indra was busy thinking of newer projects that she could take up and bring further difference to the company.

Performance with a Purpose

In 2006, Indra was a leader to watch and of course emulate. Leaders leave a great impact on people, and people like to follow what they do rather than what they say. A leader has to be aware of the kind of shadows he or she leaves behind. Indra says that a good leader has ability to create a vision, has courage of his conviction and unleash the power of people. She says that she will define a leader by these scales. By this time, Indra had introduced the vision 'Performance with a Purpose', which was an initiative to drive a long-term growth of the company and also leave a positive imprint on the society and the environment.

Going by the scale of creating a vision, she says that it is important to create a vision for you and also communicate it to those you lead. "After all, it's easier to get somewhere if you know where you are headed."

She says that the courage of the conviction comes from the research and study that a leader does. Whenever a person takes over a new important job, it is but natural for him or her to have anxiety if he/she would be able to do justice to that position. This anxiety should be primarily faced with gaining inside knowledge about what he or she is going to do. She also advises that you may have anxieties inside, but "to the company I had to project confidence, optimism, a can-do spirit and a must-do resolve". She goes on to advise further that if you want to be a leader, you got to be honest. "The one thing I've learned is don't lie to the people. Don't tell your people one thing when the reality is different."

Indra opines that leaders need to communicate to the followers; you should divulge your plans to those who matter. The plans should be classified into different layers. She says: "I told them they needed to just keep the performance going in the short-term. The medium-term focus was on what kind of acquisitions we were going to make to bolster the company's portfolio in emerging and developing markets. For the long-term, we were going to invest in R&D, start the portfolio transformation to put in place multiple initiatives which will not pay out today, but require investment today to pay out in the long-term."

She also admits that she was not sure if people would buy into her plans. To her surprise, people did and were relieved because they saw the changing trends and her plans addressed them. Her shared vision helped everyone understand where the PepsiCo was headed next.

Having the courage of conviction is also important for a leader, but that's not always easy, especially when it involves a lot of money. This makes it important for a leader to do research, listen to the concerns of others, and then using that information to make a decision. Indra had courage of conviction in enough measure, and it helped her sail through difficult presentations when the company was required to make huge investments. Her research and study stood by her in such tough times. You can't succeed with people if you haven't done your homework. She says: "You develop the courage of your convictions by listening to and addressing all concerns and gaining an additional know-how to address any skeptics."

And the last quality that a leader must possess, as per Indra, is to unleash the power of your people. It is a well-known fact that the most successful companies have a culture in which every person feels valued, no matter what his or her position is, and this helps him or her to think that he or she can make a contribution to the company.

Indra drives a culture of recognition and diversity. She knows how leveraging the power of recognition leads to positive results. The PepsiCo boosts of a number of recognition programmes for the employees and other people associated with it, and Indra derives the most satisfaction from writing letters to the parents of the team members. She says: "I tell the parents what a great job their son or daughter is doing. That recognition is worth more than money, stock runs, hugs, tickets – anything, because at the end of the day, when your parents say to you, 'I'm so proud of you, your boss just wrote to me saying you are awesome', the look on their face is worth more than one million dollars."

She says that this helped her create a terrific bond with her workers. She says: "I did not do this for them, rather I did this because I felt that the company ought to be run this way."

We should again point out these three qualities that Indra professes that can create a great leader: create a vision, find courage in your convictions, and unleash the power of your people.

Looking at the heritage she left behind, Indra says referring to the last six years with the PepsiCo: "I would like to say that I groomed almost nine CEOs for the global industry. It is a massive heritage, because you can say that you selected those people, prepared them, guided them and they went on to become CEOs of their own kind." She further says that she could have retained all of these in the PepsiCo, but it was no more possible as they had massive opportunities before them. She feels pride when she sees these people progressing in life; she feels that they are like her own children who are out in the open world doing great things. It is much like the joy of a teacher who is pleased when he finds his pupils doing well in life.

How intensely Indra feels for her employees can be known from the fact that she speaks about them in almost every interview. Contrary to what others feel, she feels that the employees are at first mother, father, uncle, aunt, sibling, neighbour and community member first, and only then they are the PepsiCo's employees. She also differs from others who say that an employee should discard the garb of her family before entering the company premises. She feels the other way round. She says: "The employees should enter the company premises with all their identities; they should not discard the individual-self at the gate and pretend to be someone else at work, and we hope that they would take the employee-self with them." She says that the whole personality should move together, and not in part. She acknowledges the fact that an employee brings to office any problem that he is facing at home. In such a scenario, it becomes the duty of the boss to talk to him and find out avenues how he can be helped.

Indra adopted several tactics to ensure the loyalty of her workers. She says that it is incumbent upon the officer to know what each member is feeling. Citing how she works, she says that in a meeting, if she finds a person sitting by himself speaking less, or looking down, she will stop the meeting for a while and ask the person to come to her office and speak his heart out. This ensured that he placed before her all the burden that he was facing, and would also feel that the CEO thinks so much about him; this strengthened his connection with the company.

❑❑

7

Gaining the Top Brass

Any success story is not the exclusive story of an individual, many other people also contribute in it. They include family members and all those who imbibe values, give support and work in a coordinated manner. Indra rose to become the President, but her is colleague Steven S. Reinemund was a step ahead of her; he had earned the position of the Board Chair and CEO (Chief Executive Officer). When he was informed about his promotion, he said that would not like to be promoted without Indra as his second in command. With their individual capabilities, the two made a perfect management team. While Indra thought strategically taking the entire picture in view, Steven had great operational experience. They had started out together as two distinct personalities, to the extent of being opposite to each other, but their open perspectives proved that each one of the two could have an enhanced value when together, and this was what made them stick together. As they came to know each other better, they formed a great team, envied by even more successful corporate in the US.

Indra's focus was simple, she wanted the PepsiCo to serve one meal or snack at each hour of day or night. As the range of products expanded, the company's rivalry was no more limited to the Coca-Cola, it was competing with a horde of companies that were in the food segment. The impressive range of products with the PepsiCo included snacks and beverages, other than the basic soft drinks for which it is known, including Mountain Dew, Rice-e-Roni, Captain Crunch, Gatorade sports drinks, Doritos and Aquafina, and others. The two together were making an effort to gain a win-win situation with a focus on health and to bring out a different mix and a much more consistent range of products.

Indra and Steven together wanted to make the PepsiCo a giant to be reckoned with in those markets in which it was not represented. For example, the initial brands of the company had been successful in the suburban regions and now they were turning focus towards the urban areas. Steven once said: “We’re a very good suburban-oriented marketing company; that’s we’ve grown over time, but there’s a huge opportunity in urban markets.”

Acknowledging Steven’s contribution regarding the expanding range of products, Indra says that the real thinking on health and wellness started in 1996-97, and it was accelerated by Steven. When you have a large established company under your command, you cannot just take a step that could be called too radical; any step has to take cognizance of the fact that the basic structure and infrastructure of the company are well utilised while going for a change in the nature of products. At her personal level, Indra wanted to enhance focus on health and wellness of the people; that is, the products which people enjoy and at the same time, which are good for their health.

Indra was thinking in the direction of bringing about a change on the company’s emphasis, but the PepsiCo was (and is) better known for its soft drinks which fall in the category of ‘fun snacks’, and which reign 70% of the company’s business and was still growing. So, paying less attention to this segment could prove disastrous for the company; and the only course open for Indra was to raise the health and wellness products rather than bring down what was selling best. She says: "So as long as that keeps growing, you will never be able to catch up easily unless you do something big."

The market survey revealed that the customer was happy with the soft drinks; many of them retorting that the company should not dare tell them what to eat and what to leave. Indra goes on to say: "That means, we have to be careful…we can improve 'fun for you', but then, I think there is always a place for those products."

Indra says that the ideal ratio between the 'fun for you' and 'good for you' products should be 50-50, but in reality, the ratio was then 70-30. The dream has to catch up with real hard facts, and the fact was that the 'fun for you' range of products were doing well, growing at a rate that is hard to catch up. In her words: "Not because we can't grow 'good for you', but because 70% of the portfolio is growing still at a rate that is going to make it hard for us to grow 'good for you' to catch up and re-balance this equation."

Indra tells the ideal situation in these words: "We want to be viewed as not just a lifestyle company that brings a slice of joy to you but also as a nutritionally responsible company. That has been our acquisition trajectory over the last few years and I think all our innovation, our strategic direction is headed that way."

She says in another interview: "With the aging population, and with everyone's focus on health, products that are nutritiously good, or nutritionally better than anything else out there, are a huge opportunity. These categories are growing several times faster than anything else."

Indra is very particular that the health concerns are answered without a compromise on taste. She says: "I'm providing the same great taste: that's the common denominator, so you don't have to make a choice between health and taste. We can bring the best of our products, and make them affordable and available because of our scale, but then we bring you nutrition credentials as well."

Indra is curious that people don't overeat unhealthy snacks all the time in the category of 'fun for you' she also wants that they are able to get healthy alternatives; this type of thinking was an important part of her strategic thinking. In an interview she appeared confident that she was concerned with people's health. She said: "I look at our portfolio and say, 'thank God for us'. I mean, I look at zero calorie SoBe Life Water, I look at G2, half the calorie. I look at these Chinese herbal medicine drinks…these are all incredible products; Naked Juice, the ultimate, good-for-you product; Quaker Oats. I look at all of our products. Stila bars from Mexico, which are whole-grain bars. I look at all this and go, 'thank God for companies like PepsiCo, which are making a difference to their portfolio and we're providing great tasting products."

She further says that taste is equally important for a snack. A consumer would not like to eat something which tastes like cardboard. She adds: "These are all great tasting products. And we're still reducing salt, reducing sugar, frying our products in hot, healthy oil. I think we're doing a great job at transforming our portfolio and I wish every food and beverage company was the same."

Explaining her philosophy about healthiness and happiness of the society, Indra says that the companies have their responsibilities towards the society and the country in which they are functioning. This responsibility goes beyond simply a company delivering its products, rather it has to deliver the products with a purpose in the mind. Also, companies are big drivers of the national and global economy. In her words: "Out of the hundred most powerful economic entities, one-third of them are companies. You know the size of big multinationals. I mean I look at our company with a market capital of $100 billion, that is pretty significant. Se we have a profound influence in society—we shape lifestyles, we shape behaviours, the interactive community. And this is not new. This is what PepsiCo has been doing for the past few years. I think I am just putting some more shape and direction to it."

With her years at the helm, Indra has helped the PepsiCo to rise and occupy a place of prestige among the defining corporations, including its listing at the New York Stock Exchange. It is also doing extremely well in terms of profits and operations. But such high performance does not make Indra an overconfident, complacent person, she keeps her shoes on the hard ground and says: "That is good news and bad news because there is no place to go but down if you make a mistake. We got to sustain that very high level of performance."

Indra has a great confidence in her employees and believes that the company could not have done well without their active cooperation and contribution. She also knows the importance of the family back home as well as the employees who should be looked as extended family. She feels that you must have an extended family at work to give you that balance. She also wants her employees to view themselves as part of the extended family and everybody at the company is there to help in every way possible. She has ensured that employees actually balance life and work.

So far as her personal life is concerned, we have described earlier how she accomplishes work-life balance. Paying attention to human resources, she says: "…the whole issue of talent sustainability—how do we make sure that people who come to work at PepsiCo are here not just to make a living, but to have a life—has unleashed the creativity of people." This type of care has brought several interesting proposals which have helped to make the PepsiCo a better place to work, with entwined fun and earnestness.

She also knows the importance of a strong competitor like Coke. He says: "…if you have no competition, a company will atrophy."

Indra remained President of the PepsiCo for three years, and during this period she ensured a spectacular performance on the financial front while doing good with the quality of the products. Her high performance was sure to bring in high rewards, it would be like breaking the glass ceiling, which is both transparent and fragile, but this becomes visible when you have focussed on it. This year was 2006. She was destined to head the company now.

❑❑

8

At the Helm

Indra had left a great impression on the PepsiCo ever since she joined it in 1994, rising through the ranks, she was now a candidate to be at the helm. The board had two choices before it, the other being co-CFO Michael D. White. If she became the CEO, she would be the first woman to head a multinational corporation of enormous size, and above that, she would be an Indian. She had left a great impression through her hard work and dedication, way of working, as well as through her dressing sense blended with Indian traditional and modern wear. As she waited outside the board room, she fancied that her mother would pray for her at this crucial time, because Shantha often claimed that her rise was chiefly due to her prayers, and not due to the long time that she kept sitting in the meeting rooms. Thinking this vapourised her stress to a great deal and she smiled to herself. In her heart, she was a little under-confident too thinking if she would be able to do well at the top post.

The board had a tough task before it. Michael D. White, the other candidate, too had performed excellently; he loved music as did Indra. And above all, they were great friends. He was an experienced colleague who looked after operations, and he was a wealth in case the company sailed in rough waters.

Finally, the board of directors decided in Indra's favour on 1 October, 2006. As soon as Indra came to know of this decision, she went to meet White in Cape Cod where he was vacationing. She did not want that a crucial member of the team should have anything against her. After all, a leader is what the constituent members make, and Indra could not overlook White. She succeeded to convince White that he would continue with the PepsiCo. She also asked the board to increase his compensation to nearly match hers. Not only this, she ensured that White was seated to her right in the board meetings.

The mutual respect the two have for each other is worth noticing. White commented, "I play the piano and Indra sings." In her turn, Indra said, "I treat Mike as my partner. He could easily have been the CEO."

Indra knows her mind well. She says: "I think to be a CEO is a calling. You should not do it because it is a job. It is a calling and you have got to be involved in it with your head, heart and hands. Your heart has got to be in the job, you got to love what you do, it consumes you. And if you are not willing to get into the CEO job that way, there is no point getting into it. And I love the job. I love the company, I love the people, I loved it when I was president and love it as much as CEO."

How she loves the PepsiCo is evident from what she says: "[If I wasn't working at PepsiCo] I would be applying for a job to come to PepsiCo! I feel like I am home. I'm serious when I say that I would be trying to be part of a company like PepsiCo or trying to change the environment in some other company so it looks more like PepsiCo."

When asked how she was going to tackle the situation on work front and home front, she says: "I want to make something even bigger of this company than it was and what I have to do is decide every moment in time whether I am going to be a mother or a wife or an executive. It's a day-to-day thing."

It would be like revelation to know that Indra Nooyi is penning a book. This could not be an ordinary occurrence as many other CEOs and all those who have become folk heroes in the eyes of people do. Her new book will focus on a matter that is beyond the business concerns: How to integrate work and family without short-changing either. From this we can know how great importance she attaches to the role of family in a professional setting. It is an issue that tens of millions of individuals grapple with everyday. And as a wife and mother, Indra has faced this situation while being at the helm of affairs of a company that has 260,000 employees the world over.

Indra knows the importance of the employees and sees them as part of her extended family. She says: "The thing I like about PepsiCo is the team that has been built, the culture that exists, a sort of ownership culture. It is extraordinary. I think that's what makes the difference. I always tell my people that what I never want to do is, if they get a competing offer from some other company, to match it and then hold on to them. At that point, I have lost their hearts."

For her, dedication also involves loyalty to the company. On one occasion, she says: "When a head hunter calls, I don't want to take the call. I want to say, I love this company so much that I won't take the call. That's what we need to do. Because ultimately it is the people that are going to make or break the company, it is not the assets, it is not the brand." She knows well that an employee can be happy only when his family is happy. This is the reason that she likes to interact with them. She says: "I like to support my team's families because my own career has been tough on my own family."

Functioning at the top, Indra feels no dearth of new ideas which she could execute in her domain as the CEO. She has stated an intent to develop a line of snacks marketed specifically for women, feeling that it is hitherto unexplored category. In a radio interview, she says: "PepsiCo is getting ready to launch products designed and package accordance to women's preferences, and based on behavioural differences in the way men and women consume snacks.

On 6 August, 2018, the PepsiCo confirmed that Indra K. Nooyi would step down as CEO. She was replaced with Ramon Laguarta, a 22-year veteran of the company. Indra continued to serve as the Chairman till early 2019. During her tenure as the CEO, the company's sales grew 80%. She served as CEO for 12 years, 7 years longer than the average CEO tenure at large companies. When she was asked if there was a debate on the board about structural changes and if that discussion influenced her decision to leave the PepsiCo, she said: "I've been in the company 24 years and I've been CEO for 12. Twelve years. That's way past the average tenure of any CEO. I started a discussion about a year ago saying 'You know what? It's time to make the change.' Twelve years is a long time, and I'd like to do something different with my life and let's talk about how to effect an orderly transition."

When it was time for Indra to gracefully climb down the helm, what she had achieved was simply splendid. Today, the PepsiCo is the second most recognised beverage brand in the world, after Coke, and several of its other brands, including Tropicana, Gatorade and Quaker Oats are billion-dollar businesses in their own right. Indra's tenure, above all, brought confidence in the customers that the drinks and snacks are safe, and that the taste of them, that irresistible combination of flavours, will be the same every time. She also succeeded in making the brands in abstract and aspirational terms going beyond the company's culture and its mission, as defined by Indra Nooyi. She is quite clear in her mind when she says that it is not enough to make things that taste good, PepsiCo must also be a good company. It must aspire to higher values than the day-to-day business of making and selling soft drinks and snacks. And as you know, Indra calls this

'Performance with a Purpose' which is well a screensaver on the company's computers.

When she was questioned what she would like to do next, she did not open her cards and said: "No idea. If you have any ideas, let me know. Right now, what I'm focussed on is seeing the CEO job…[after which] I'm making a trip with my mum and the family. My mother's old. And then decide what to do sometime in early 2019. I haven't thought beyond the CEO job at this point. But I do know I want to do something different."

She was also asked at this point of time if she asked for more time from the board, she said: "The interesting thing about PepsiCo is the day you become CEO, you start the succession process because you have to think about emergency succession. We do that in a very deliberate way. So the conversation I had with the board about me transitioning out of the company was a very very sensible, responsible structured discussion."

Speaking about the effect her leaving the PepsiCo would mean for the company and if it will change the direction, structure or potential structure of the company, Indra said: "That's for Ramon [Laguarta] to decide. Let him take his time. Let him form a point of view. The only thing I would say is he should do whatever he thinks is right for the company. He's a very good executive. He will do what's right for the company and whatever he chooses to do, I will support him."

When asked about her biggest achievement in the PepsiCo, Indra said with a smile: "We transformed PepsiCo. Our product portfolio went from mostly 'fun for you' products to 'fun for you', 'better for you', 'good for you'. Becoming a much more responsible environmental steward. Reducing water usage, increasing recycling rate, reducing our carbon footprint. That's what we set out to do; and doing all this, we also said we want to deliver short-term results. We threaded the needle between performance and purpose and delivered terrific earnings per share performance growth."

Indra said in response to the question about her biggest disappointment thus: "If we didn't have the great financial recession, we could have started the journey faster. Second that activists have a role to play in the industry. Sometimes they are constructive, sometimes they are not. In our case, they were constructive. But all I'll tell you is that if we didn't have to be distracted by activists etc., we would have continued on our path in a much more deliberate and a more accelerated way. But you know what? I have no regrets because activists made us better people, made us look at our portfolio even more critically. So at the end of the day, for any CEO, we want to do things faster. I would have loved to have done things faster."

In 2019, Indra became the co-director of the newly created Connecticut Economic Resource Center, a public-private partnership with the Connecticut Department of Economic and Community Development. She will help draft the state's new development strategy.

Nooyi also serves on the boards of the International Cricket Council and several non-profit organisations, including the US-India Business Council, the Consumer Goods Forum, Catalyst, Lincoln Center for the Performing Arts, Tsinghua University School of Economics and Management, the World Economic Forum and the Asia Society.

Indra has also been in the forefront for fighting the pandemic Covid-19. In April 2020, it was announced that she and the Yale epidemiologist Dr. Albert Ko will represent Connecticut on the six-state working group planning for the careful easing of Covid-19 restrictions. The two will co-chair the Reopen Connecticut Advisory Group.

She is also the co-chair of a non-profit organisation called AdvanceCT, based at Connecticut. She is also a member of several organisations, including the board of directors at Amazon. She also believes in philanthropy. In 2016, she gifted an undisclosed amount to her alma mater: the Yale School of Management. She became the school's biggest alumni donor in history and the first woman to endow a deanship at a top school with her gift. She and her husband Raj together donated 187,000 Scholastic books to Connecticut's alliance school districts as part of the Partnership for Connecticut during the Covid-19 crisis.

Indra has been conferred with a large number of awards and recognitions, including honorary degrees by several universities. The highest award for her was the Padma Bhushan which was awarded by the President of India in 2007 for her exceptional work in the international arena. Indra had created history when she became one among the few India-born females to lead a global giant when she took over the reins at PepsiCo.

Indra feels grateful to America where any person coming from any other country can realize his dreams. Many lament that the dreams of the newcomers to the US are myths that cannot be realized, but her career trajectory provides testimony that the door of opportunity is still open and that merit still matters.

❑❑

9

In the Mind

The mind determines what kind a person is. During the course of this book, we have included a large number of extracts from what Indra K. Nooyi said in the interviews with newspapers, radio and TV channels and others. What made this author a fan of hers was that she can speak forthrightly without caring for the impact, and that's why she is called honest. She expresses her opinions very frankly, as she did when Clinton lost the elections in 2016 and Trump became the American President. She said on this occasion: "Clinton's loss left my daughters and PepsiCo's employees devastated and there were serious concerns among the company's workers, especially the non-white employees, about their safety in an America with Donald Trump as its President."

The Yale SOM's Jeffrey Sonnenfield wrote in a blog post that Nooyi brought a rare combination of intelligence, toughness and vision to the job. He writes: "She has shown time and again that she thinks profoundly. She has often demonstrated how leaders can be tough and persuasive without being abusive. She does not allow to make a gender caricature of her leadership style, and through diplomacy, she has won over predecessors, colleagues, and even once-hostile activist investors."

In support of his contention, Jeffrey cites an incident: "An example of this is when she proved out her vision to once-skeptical activist investor Nelson Peltz and his firm Trian Partners. In 2013, they bought a stake in PepsiCo and launched a hostile campaign demanding that Frito Lay snacks be divested from Pepsi's beverage business. They also said the beverage business in North America be divested from the beverage business in the rest of the world. Nooyi believed in her integrated, brand-building vision with intertwined distribution channels, but welcomed a Trian representative to the board and became friends with Peltz. Three years later, Trian sold their holdings for a remarkable 67% gain—a result of Nooyi's vision."

Heritage and pride in the past is a good thing for a company, but Indra has shown that the old companies, like PepsiCo, don't have to live in the past. She adopted several practices which deviated from the past legacy and showed that these can work effectively. She hired a specialist endocrinologist and obesity expert to help revolutionise the nutritional base of the company's old and new products. In the past, 75% of the company's products were in the less healthy category of 'fun for you', after her tenure at the helm, PepsiCo's tasty 'good for you' snacks make half of the product portfolio. Every two years during her tenure, the company has created a new $1 million+ brand business, moving from 16 to 22 mega brands.

Indra has also shown that the presumed trade-off between short-term financial returns and long-term investing is a false choice. Through her 'performance with a purpose' mission, she has shown that doing good is not antithetical to doing well. She has led the industry in a responsible water use, ended the use of trans fats and dramatically reduced sugar in PepsiCo's products. She also introduced recyclable packaging and achieved other inspiring sustainable and nutritional milestones aimed at helping communities and customers.

Dietary balance has been a key feature of Indra's strategy since day one. In 2010, she declared that Pepsi needed to be part of the solution to 'one of the world's public health challenges'; when she said this, she meant a challenge which was basically linked to her industry.

obesity. Under her steer, Pepsi has reduced the portion sizes of its 'fun for you' products and has delivered a marketing campaign to ensure its 'diet' products are promoted as vigorously as its full-sugar equivalents. For example, Gatorade is now specifically marketed towards athletes, rather than being advertised as an everyday recreational beverage.

Today, the PepsiCo has a diversified portfolio of products. It still sells sugary drinks and potato chips, but it also has Tropicana, Naked Juice and Izze supporting the healthier end of its range. Since her joining the PepsiCo, she has also set Pepsi on a drive to reduce the salt, sugar and fat contents in its core products, while at the same time, ramping up the production of its 'good for you' offerings, largely in response to the demands of modern society. She says: "Our company's business was developed in a different time. As society became more sedentary, the offering of food and beverages to that society had to change. There is a time and place for fun products, but now increasingly we have to develop good-for-you products that are suitable for an increasingly sedentary population."

Realizing her duty towards shareholders, community and societies around the world, she says: "At the end of the day, companies like ours are little republics. PepsiCo's market capitalisation makes us bigger than many countries around the world. Companies like ours have not only got [to be] run for the benefit of shareholders. We've got to do it in a way that's very sensitive to societies and communities around the world. And that's my sincere hope that every company views their place in the society that way, and modifies [its] business model to be more sensitive to those countries, societies and communities in which they operate."

On another occasion, she avails the opportunity to say in this regard: "Large companies are powerful, they can play a big role, so we need to work with governments to provide solutions. The real challenge is, instead of sitting down and figuring out who is responsible, specifically, why don't we say we need to be part of the solution?"

While Indra applied new ideas to the old practices, she ensured that none of these societal triumphs were at the expense of the shareholder's wealth; the total shareholder return came to 162% as compared with 130% of the competitors. The PepsiCo shares have more than doubled the rise of the arch rival Coca-Cola. When Indra took over, the earnings were $35 billion and it was $63.5 billion in the last year of her term, with the company's price nearly doubling in that period.

The Indra's greatest achievement of Indra is that she has reached prominence without self-promotion. She has towered over the Forbes and the Fortune lists of the most powerful leaders (not to mention the most powerful women leaders), while winning every award in her industry. Her way of working is also rooted to the ground. Rather than choosing to go for hagiographic profiles and grandiose press releases, she herself travels the whole of America and the world talking about the PepsiCo's collective goals.

In 2008, Indra was elected the Chair of the US India Business Council, which was brought into existence to create an inclusive bilateral trade environment between India and the US by serving as the voice of the industry, linking governments to businesses and supporting long-term commercial partnerships that will nurture the spirit of entrepreneurship, create jobs and successfully contribute to the global economy. As a recognition of her work on the council, she was presented with the 2015 Global Leadership Award for her commitment to driving a more inclusive global economy and encouraging the creation of more roles for female leaders.

Indra is also open to innovation in design and marketing. She branded Pepsi in a new avatar. For this, she sought the help of Mauro Porcini, an Italian design expert, and assigned him the task of rebranding and reinventing one of the world's most recognisable brands. Today, the PepsiCo is pushing the design through the entire system, from product creation to packaging and labelling, to how the product looks on the shelf, and how Pepsi's consumers will interact with it.

Rather than focussing on the product's face, Indra initiated an altogether new approach to marketing. For instance, one of the project's new creations is the Pepsi Spire, a unique touch-screen fountain vending machine. While competitors' vending machines have focussed on adding a few more buttons and different combination of flavours, Pepsi has created a fundamentally different interaction between consumer and machine. The Spire is essentially a large iPad that communicates with the consumer, giving invitation to interact with it. It tracks the customer's habits, so that when a consumer swipes his ID, the machine reminds him of the flavour combinations he tried last time and suggests new ones, while attractive graphic work continues on the screen.

The PepsiCo is currently the second largest food and beverage company in the world, boasting about $63 billion in revenues. Many people are inclined to give Indra the credit for this performance who has consistently taken the company in a profit-making direction.

When Indra left the PepsiCo, it was the world leader in global salty snack sales, and it comes second in the sale of beverage. This is testimony to the success of her marketing and positional strategies. The most notable thing about her work is that she has made these products healthier. Over decades, the full-calorie soda sales were at their peak in 1960s and towards late 1990s, and ever since, due to increasing awareness of consumers towards healthier options, the sales of the main brands have suffered. Indra saw this trend that the depreciation would sustain over the years. She found that the consumers were now turning towards healthier products like energy drinks, bottled water and coffee; and sale has spiked in these segments. Indra took this opportunity to conjoin her emphasis on healthier foods under 'good for you' scheme to focus on healthier products and beverages.

We cannot deny the fact that the revenues of the PepsiCo have grown over a hundred times during the past fifty years, and with this, despite its sense of high purpose, a public-health crisis has been steadily growing as people are getting fatter. The trend which started in the US and the world in 1980s, it has reached epidemic proportions in the next two decades. Many studies have found that high-calorie, low-cost processed foods and drinks as one of the major drivers of obesity around the world. Snacks, in particular, play a role in childhood obesity which is growing even faster than obesity in adults. People consume soft drinks several times of what they consumed four decades ago, and due to these tasty snacks, they ingest sodium almost double that of the recommended dose, which is closely linked to high blood pressure; add to this the use of oils and fats used in some fried potato and corn chips which raise the cholesterol level and can cause heart disease. In other words, the 'high purpose' brands of the PepsiCo rely more on sugar, salt and fats, and they appear to be making people sick; and the funniest thing is that the 'heavy users', as the devoted fans are called in industry, could be among the worst afflicted. Cutting short the lives of your best customers can in no way be called the best strategy.

For her work and accomplishments Indra has been rewarded handsomely. From 2007 until 2014, Forbes listed her in its World's 100 Most Powerful Women, while Fortune named her number one on its annual ranking of Most Powerful Women in Business in 2006-2010. In 2008, the US New & World Report named her one of America's best leaders. Her zeal for high accomplishment can be gauged from her statement: "We ought to keep pushing the boundaries to get to flawless execution. Flawless is the ultimate goal."

Indra also conducted programmes to bring Pepsi closer to people. In 2010, it started the Pepsi Refresh Project spending a $20 million advertising budget on a social media campaign. Under this, the customers submitted their ideas to Pepsi for ways to refresh their communities with the proclaimed aim of 'making the world a better place'; and as an outcome, the PepsiCo funded the projects which garnered the most number of votes. This has resulted in disbursal of over $20 million on diverse worthy causes including health, arts and culture, food and shelter, education and others. This movement helped the customers to feel a kind of kinship with Pepsi and it emerged as a forward-thinking, innovative brand. Indra wanted to build this type of kinship right from the day she emerged at the helm of affairs.

Indra was never afraid of criticism. When she turned the company product portfolio towards healthier products, she was scoffed at. She describes this in an interesting manner: "They kept telling me, 'Why are you Mother Teresa? Why are you trying to change your portfolio to healthier products?' Because that's where the market was going. That's where we needed to go."

She opines that both CEOs of public corporations and their shareholders need to have better dialogues around strategy. "And that's not to say that keeping an eye on the quarterly results is bad, but it becomes toxic to the company's future value when it's the only thing that matters." With an emphasis, she says: "…if you're doing something truly strategic and transformative, it always evokes criticism."

She also makes out how difficult it is to deviate from the existing product portfolio: "Will your competitors challenge you at every point in time? In my industry they do. Where I said lower the sugar levels, go to a different product portfolio, they doubled down on sugar drinks. So what do you do? You lose share, you give up some share. That's ok. Because we played a different portfolio game. But educating the investor world is difficult. It requires enormous courage, conviction, consistency. It is painful, very painful."

When she went for the quality change of the product portfolio, she was courageous. She says: "…consumer tastes change all the time. They change in food and beverage faster than they change any where else. This was a great opportunity for us to change our portfolio, go where the consumer's going and gain market share. But it was not stupid enough to say this can be done overnight. I knew this journey was going to be arduous."

Speaking about a woman being at the top, Indra says: "Women are searching for role models. They want to talk to people who've made it to the CEO suite to learn how they've operated in a more male setting. How did they trade off having families and the job? Then a lot of diverse people turn to me to say, 'Tell me as an immigrant woman, how did you move forward in an American business context?' Then I have a lot of demands from Indian-American people who say, 'Can you tell us how Indian-Americans can move forward in a global business environment?' I get the tug and pull from all three constituencies."

Unfolding her heart about being lonely at the top, she admits that it's incredibly lonely there. Of course, I add, you are accompanied by glory, and Indra, you got a good measure of that. Good wishes!

❑❑